To Sue,

Best Wishes
on Taking The Best
& Highest Road In Your
Life.

All The Best,

Adam

*Alan Holube*sko

Taking the Great High Road

AN EXPLORATION AND WORKABLE
PERSPECTIVE OF CHARACTER BUILDING

Holubesko, Alan
   Taking the Great High Road -- An Exploration and
   Workable Perspective of Character Building. Library of
   Congress Card No. 95-96193. $17.95
ISBN: 0-9650413-0-1

A&L Publishing
PO Box 43
Norwich, CT 06360 USA
860-889-0006

Produced, published and printed in the United States of America.

Alan Holubesko

Taking the Great High Road

AN EXPLORATION AND WORKABLE PERSPECTIVE OF CHARACTER BUILDING

How would you like to be in the same league as Abraham Lincoln?

Achieve true success by applying seven components of character building.

A study in integrity by utilizing the power to do good.

Discover your own happiness by making others happy.

Dedication

I would like to dedicate this book to my wife, Linda, who has loved me all these years, and for her support in my commitment to complete this endeavor.

Alan Holubesko

Table of Contents

INTENTIONALLY LEFT BLANK

Alan Holubesko

Author's Statement

Why did I write this book? My father always used to say that the world is made up of two kinds of people. There are leaders and there are followers. My experience has afforded the opportunity to be part of both categories. Under the right conditions being a boss or a follower can be a good thing. Conversely, if the opposite is true, either category can be a nightmare.

I have always pondered over the adversarial relationship between all living things. One sees it all through the animal kingdom. It seems to be a fact of nature. The same condition exists with us humans. Competition and strife always seems to win out over meekness and gentleness. It appears one must be ruthless to get anywhere in this life.

I asked my father about that very fact one time. His reply was: "That's just the way the world is, you can't change it."

His reply has perplexed me for over twenty-five years. Do nice guys always finish last? What do you mean; you can't

i

change it? Why must there be strife between management and labor? Why can't husbands and wives get along? Why is the generation gap expanding? Why does it always have to be "me first" all the time? Why do people use power to lord over others instead of helping each other? There are many other questions one could pose in this vein. It would appear, in order for one to succeed, one must play the game according to the rules of the jungle. Survival of the fittest is the rule. Watch out for "number one," and forget about everybody else. Is it any wonder why the world is in its present condition?

Does this mean we are in a race to garner as much as possible in the ways of the world such as: power, wealth, and "one upsmanship?" We run to and fro heading to nowhere. There must be a better way.

A number of years ago, I worked for a large retail jewelry firm. After many years of clawing my way up the corporate ladder I decided to give it all up! There were several reasons for my decision. The deciding factor consisted of observing and analyzing my colleagues who were roughly five years ahead of me in the corporate hierarchy. The good news was the high salary, beautiful home in the suburb, nice cars, and the illusion of security. It did not mean that any of this was wrong or bad, it was merely a matter of motivation. The bad news was young men and women growing old before their time. Deteriorating health in the form of ulcers, diabetes, heart disease, cancer and alcoholism, was all too common. All of these, as a direct result of years of pressure to produce or you'll be out! The higher up one went, the more time would be spent on long and frequent business trips. Being away from home and family resulted in all kinds of difficulty and eventual collapse of the "American Dream."

What does one do when it seems like the whole world seems to be closing on them? What does one do when one feels surrounded by all sorts of pressures? There is an answer to this sort of hopeless feeling. Someone else always has it worse than you, and is in the process of working out of the situation.

This reminds me of a story. While in "boot camp," in the Marine Corps, we were constantly encouraged by heroic deeds of those who preceded us. General "Chesty" (because of all his medals) Puller, was the most decorated soldier in the history of the Marine Corps. He fought in several wars culminating with the Korean Conflict. The famous battle of the Chosin Reservoir also known as the "Frozen Chosin," was a high point in Marine Corps battle anals. The Marines and other Allied troops found themselves hemmed-in and surrounded by a great number of Chinese troops. With no reinforcements in sight, the situation appeared hopeless. A paraphrased version of the account goes like this:

A frightened young Marine approached General Puller during the bleakest part of the whole affair and asked Puller the following question: "General, they've got us surrounded, what are we going to do?" Puller pondered briefly and offered the young man this consolation. "Son, we've got 'em right where we want 'em. Now get back to the line and hold your position!"

Eventually, they did fight their way out. That's the point! No matter how hopeless it may seem. Whatever the "Chosin Reservoir" is in your life, if you are surrounded by difficulty, the only solution is to hang tough and fight your way out! The big question is this: If there were a way to succeed in every facet of life, regardless if one is a follower or a leader, would it be worth investigating? The answer is a resounding YES! In my years of menial labor, sales management, entrepreneur, educator, writer, television producer, and communicator, I have found that there must exist in one's character a number of key components or traits woven together by a single motivating concept.

It is hoped that this book will help those who have wondered what the true meaning of success really encompasses. The principles that follow, do work. As with any knowledge, if it is not applied it is useless.

∂Acknowledgments

I would like to thank all those who preceded me in publishing various works on Abraham Lincoln. Their efforts to preserve and chronicle historical information is invaluable.

Special thanks to Alonzo Rothschild who produced a wonderful compilation on Lincoln's honesty. I am greatly appreciative for Dale Carnegie's book on "Lincoln the Unknown." It gave me insight and a foundational perspective by which to demythologize Lincoln. I am also appreciative of Keith W. Jennison who authored "The Humorous Mr. Lincoln," without such, it would have been difficult to complete the chapter on humor. I am also deeply indebted as a researcher to Barnes & Noble Books for their 1992 edition of "The Living Lincoln." This compilation of Lincoln's own writings gave me the inspiration that has led to this

---

labor of love. The biographical work of Ida M. Tarbell and William Elroy Curtis also contributed to my deeper understanding of President Lincoln.

I would like to thank my wife Linda, who helped me in the area of research and editing. I would also like to thank Janie Carlisle for her technical expertise and advice concerning the publishing of this effort.

I wish to thank my friends: Jack and Pat Brogan, who were instrumental in helping me to embark on the great high road. For Mary Moon, and Elaine Peterson for touching my life in a special way, which has contributed to the completion of this work.

Finally, I wish to thank God the creator of this universe for strengthening me when I needed it most, and helping me to persevere under pressure.

𝔓reface

WHAT YOU WILL LEARN FROM READING THIS BOOK

Did you ever ask yourself: Who am I? Where am I going? Am I a success in life? What is success anyway? Does it mean I need to end up as a CEO of a giant corporation, or President of the United States?

We all start out in this life with a clean slate. Some of us go on to attain great acomplishments, while most go on to lead lives in the mediocrity of quiet desperation. We get by, but life takes on a subtle routine of boredom and endless trials. We read of those who overcame tremendous adversity and climbed out of the depths of deprivation to accomplish great feats of success. Athletes are making millions. Rock stars are making millions. A lucky Lotto player hits the jackpot for millions. Where do the rest of us fit in? Can a person achieve a measure of success in his or her own right, with a richness and uniqueness that is unequaled?

There comes a time in a person's life when a period of assessment becomes apparent. This usually happens around middle age. One is about half-way through life, and begins to wonder where they have been, and where they are going? In this age of high technology and "downsizing," the old staples of stability are shaken. It's hard to feel successful if you're an engineer who is forty-five and just got laid-off. It's hard to feel successful when that special spark no longer flickers in a marriage. For many, a period of assessment happens much earlier.

The years of adolescence bring on problems with growth, self esteem, and peer pressure. Today, the stakes are higher. Drug use, teen pregnancy, and crimes of all sorts are on an astronomical course. There seems to be no end in sight with little or no hope for solutions. It does not need to be this way. There is hope—to which this endeavor is dedicated.

There is a way to achieve success in every life. It cannot be measured in personal wealth or acquisition. It can only be measured by a principal of interaction dating back to the dawn of recorded history. There is a direct cause and effect relationship concerning the measure of success on how well people interact with each other. This interaction involves the principal of considering others before self.

Imagine a world where this was the rule as opposed to the exception. Implementing this may sound Utopian, and it's probably true. The purpose of this book is not to change the world. The world cannot change unless individuals change. As the song goes: Let there be peace and let it start with me, is where the change must begin. The fact is; considering others before oneself works! History is replete with men and women who carried this principal to astonishing heights.

A brief example concerning the above concept is a relatively insignificant leader who never made the front page of the newspaper, or ever made it into the history books. This person may have made the paper at one time or another, he certainly made the obituary column when he died. His philosophy and impact as a leader, however, is monumental.

The leader happened to be the boss of a friend of mine. She shared with me his basic concept of leadership. He was a middle manager working for the phone company. Whenever an employee would enter his office, he would greet them with the following question: "Hi, how can I make your day more pleasant?" When was the last time your boss asked you how he or she could make your day more pleasant? The philosophy prevailing today appears to be the direct opposite. Most, in a position of authority seem to relish in how they can make one's day more miserable, or simply do not have the presence of mind to truly care for others. The following example illustrates a deficit in leadership.

In my home state of Connecticut, the plight of those who served our nation in the way of military service is increasing. The ranks of those abusing drugs, constantly unemployed, homelessness, committing suicide, and requiring much needed medical attention are swelling. Tragically, women and children, as dependents, in the way of the above aforementioned, are joining the rank and file of poverty and despair.

In September of 1992, an annual effort to help needy veterans of prior military service began on the grounds of the Connecticut State Veterans Hospital, located in Rocky Hill.

For a brief period, usually a weekend, needy veterans have the opportunity to avail themselves of the many services offered. Such as: Medical exams, employment aid, etc. It is a noble effort, and has produced some wonderful results. With shrinking budgets and competing priorities, however, some are beginning to fall through the cracks. Worst yet, the gap between the clients and the administrators is widening. Why is this happening? There are a variety of reasons. The question is, what could our leaders be doing to alleviate this situation? One answer lies within a leader to commit an act of sincere caring that would not cost anyone a dime.

In the past, as a member of the Disabled American Veterans organization, I've participated as a volunteer to help in the food service portion of the annual event. As I was performing my duties, a high state official entered the dining hall and made a few rudimentary remarks. At the conclusion of his brief statement, he departed. The clients were not impressed. They could see right through the political maneuvering and patronizing lip service which many of them found offensive. The comments I overheard were disconcerting and alarming. It would have been a wonderful gesture, and prudent as a leader, for this high official to have sat down among the troops and break bread with them. This person should have taken the time to listen firsthand to their concerns and problems. Being sincere in this manner would have gained him much respect as opposed to the feelings of apathy and disrespect which permeated the air. This state official should have sincerely had the presence of mind to take advantage of his power and seize the opportunity, in order to make the day more pleasant for many people. Please do not misunderstand, the effort to help the needy veterans is very noble. My point is that our leaders on all levels of government really need to get off their high horses and roll up their shirt sleeves, and come down to the level of all their constituents.

IMAGINE IT! Ask someone as soon as possible. How can I make your day more pleasant? Ask your husband, wife, children, co-worker, etc. I guarantee one thing, the person who is on the receiving end of this question will be amicably jolted. In most cases, people will probably give you a double-take. "Is this person for real?" Then, they will be surprised at the nature of the question. Certainly, they will be even more astonished at the proposal because of your sincere desire in caring about their welfare. This simple and sincere question is profound in its ramifications. Think about it! Imagine the positive impact on people.

How can one learn to apply this success principal or as Ralph Waldo Emerson put it: the sovereignty of ethics to task? That question will be answered in the Introduction that follows.

𝔍ntro𝔡uction

A man should be a guest in his own house, and a guest in his own thought, wrote Ralph Waldo Emerson. He is there to speak for truth; but who is he? Is he one who was created for the sole purpose of gain and acquisition? Is the realization of his private interests paramount to that of the great commands of love? Can a state of happiness and productivity be achieved through a foundation built upon a solid rock of ethics and character? History reveals the answer to be yes, when the sovereignty of ethics is upheld.

Prior to the undertaking of a study in ethics and character, an understanding concerning the true definition of success must be established. Can success be measured by how many toys or accumulation of wealth one may garner? Or is there something more profound and meaningful? What affect has one's life had on others?

NOBODY GETS OUT OF HERE ALIVE! If you were given six months to live, what would you do? You would be presented with two options. First, you could crawl into a shell and wait for death. Second, you could live each day as if it were your last, redeeming the time and making the most out of life. A successful leader would choose the latter.

Most of us have opportunities to be leaders — fathers, mothers, husbands, wives, boss at work, etc. My purpose for writing this book, is to share with you eight components of character building, that will help you achieve the great high road of leadership and success, regardless of your situation in life. The question of what is true success demands an answer. True success can be defined as the accomplishment of goals realized through the process of conversion, which enables the individual to attain a state of mind foregoing private interests and regards. The motivation is to exist for the sole purpose of loving the true Author of life, and a genuine love of neighbor. In other words, taking the great high road in all actions and interactions.

What are the components of character building? What characteristics describe a person who is successful? They are honesty, candor, compassion, humor, humility, faith, love of family and country and finally, wisdom. The strengthening component that binds these eight together is the concept of esteeming others more than oneself. Key figures in history have personified these character traits to the degree of establishing astonishing results. It must be noted, however, the above character traits do not work independently of each other. They must work in concert with each other. A good example of this concerns the trait of candor. It is good for a leader to be candid with his or her subordinates, but not to the point of being destructive. To be constructive, candor must also contain the elements of compassion, love, and honesty or whatever other traits are applicable to achieve the proper results.

Though rarely realized, the human condition is occasionally graced by the likes of exceptional people who appear on the world scene of human events. The Bible is replete with men and women who accomplished extraordinary feats of success culminating with Jesus Christ. One of more recent significance such as: Abraham Lincoln, is the focus of this work.

I became very interested in the life of Lincoln in 1982 when I read a book titled: LINCOLN THE UNKNOWN, by Dale Carnegie. What captivated my interest was the way this biography really captured the essence of the man Lincoln and the way he led his life. Lincoln entered this world under the humblest of conditions. Born in the backwoods of Kentucky, and living under deplorable conditions of poverty in Indiana, his ethical foundation was not based on personal wealth or the privilege of attending the finest schools. How could a man with a formal education that was "defective," as he so aptly put it, accomplish so much? Why is Lincoln the most beloved and most written about of all the American Presidents? There are volumes of material chronicling his life. What is it about this man that is worthy of learning and appropriate for incorporating into our lives today? How would you like to achieve and be regarded in the same stature as Lincoln in your own right? The answer to the question of what made this man tick, may also be found in his own writings. The secret of his success lies within the personal thoughts he recorded as his life unfolded. Through an analysis of how he reacted to life's challenges, a pattern begins to emerge on the true meaning of success.

Before we embark on the exploration and workable perspective of taking the great high road, I call your attention to my use of parenthetical references. There are two reasons why I decided to use references throughout this work. First, to validate my research. Second, to make it easier for quick research, if one desires follow-up study.

Chapter 1
Honesty
THE BEST POLICY

Alonzo Rothschild who authored, "HONEST ABE," began by writing this: He who seeks to understand the character and achievement of Abraham Lincoln must begin with a study of the man's honesty. Being honest was very important to Lincoln. It didn't matter to him if he appeared foolish or childish. Often, it may have seemed his honesty was ludicrous in light of the situation. Between 1831-1837 Lincoln hired out as a clerk in the village store in New Salem, IL. It wasn't long before tales were told of how he walked six miles to give back a few pennies to a woman who overpaid for dry goods. His honesty bordered on the fanatical, but history shows that this rare quality in an

1

individual of great success and achievement literally saved a nation.

HONESTY IS THE BEST POLICY

In March, 1837 ("LINCOLN THE UNKOWN," Dale Carnegie, page 48-49) Lincoln departed New Salem and rode to Springfield, IL on a borrowed horse. His purpose was to begin what he called his "experiment as a lawyer." In his saddle-bag were all his earthly possessions which included several law books along with shirts and underwear. An old blue sock was stuffed with six-and-a quarter-cent and twelve-and-a-half-cent pieces of money. This was money he had collected for postage as a postmaster back in New Salem before it closed. During his first year in Springfield he needed cash often and badly. He could have spent the money and paid the Government out of his own pocket, but he would have felt that to be dishonest. Eventually, a year or two later, a Post-Office auditor finally came around for a settlement. Lincoln not only turned over the exact amount of cash, but the exact coins he took with him. Why? Because he believed to never use any money but his own.

When Lincoln first rode into Springfield, he was not only broke, but was eleven hundred dollars in debt. He and his partner lost this money due to an ill-fated grocery store venture back in New Salem. His partner, unfortunately, drank himself to death and left Lincoln holding the bag. Legally, Lincoln did not have to shoulder the entire burden because of divided responsiblity and the failure of a business. This could have afforded him with some sort of legal loophole. Oh no, not "honest Abe," that wasn't his way. Instead, he went to his creditors and promised to pay every cent. In fact, even as late as 1848, as a member of Congress, he continued to send part of his salary home to pay off the old debt.

As a nation, paying off debt is a concept that has faded into oblivion. Our national debt continues to soar into the trillions of dollars. Bankruptcies, both personal and business are at record levels. Unpaid student loans continue to mount. How can a nation continue to be blessed financially when it follows the dishonest path of forgoing personal responsibility?

TRUTH IN LAW

His handling of money was no less conscientious as a lawyer dealing with his partners or clients. ("HONEST ABE," Alonzo Rothschild, page 47) Lincoln set up a financial creed of his own. Basically, it was this, the money of another was sacred from being used by him, even temporarily. He did not want to discard the distinctive character which made up one's property. As a result, he quickly gained the confidence of his clients.

Lincoln possessed a certain attitude concerning "TRUTH IN LAW." ("HONEST ABE," Alonzo Rothschild, page 48) His office became a court of conciliation. After some fifteen years of legal experience, he believed litigation should be discouraged. "Persuade your neighbors to compromise wherever you can. Point out to them how the nominal winner is often the loser—in fees, expenses, and waste of time," Lincoln professed. "As a peacemaker the lawyer has a superior opportunity of being a good man. There will be business enough." ("THE LIVING LINCOLN") This philosophy put into practice, helped Lincoln in getting the parties to almost always submit in his settlements and arbitrations. A practice that would pay handsome dividends for him as a Presidential leader. This advice is ageless. Imagine the time, expense, and heartache that would not be required if the concept of compromise or deferring for the common good were exercised.

It is a well documented fact that we as a nation have become addicted to litigation, in order to resolve problems. It seems that many are on a constant search for ways of perpetuating lawsuits. Unfortunately, in all too many cases, attorneys welcome the business, and judges promote the scam by awarding ridiculous amounts of money to satisfy the plaintiffs and attorneys greed. It is a hidden tax which causes the rest of us to pay high premiums for insurance.

HONESTY IS A LEARNED BEHAVIOR

What is the lesson to be learned here? Why was the character trait of honesty so deeply engrained in Lincoln's psyche? Mr. Rothschild in his book, "HONEST ABE," cites Usher F. Linder who knew the Lincoln family back in Kentucky. In his eulogy to Mr. Lincoln, Mr. Linder made mention of the fact that the Lincolns were a good family. "They were poor, and the very poorest people of the middle classes, but they were true." Isn't it interesting that one of the leading causes of dishonesty noted by prominent sociologists today is poverty? Based on this kind of logic, Lincoln's honorable behavior is an enigma. A close analysis of just how poor he was is characterized by his early life in Indiana. ("LINCOLN THE UNKNOWN," Dale Carnegie, page 22) In the winter of 1816-17 the Lincoln family slept curled up like dogs on a heap of leaves and bearskins dumped on the floor in the corner of a shed, hastily built by his father. They had no butter, no milk, no eggs, no fruit, nor vegetables or potatoes. They survived mainly on wild game and nuts. So humble and poor was their lot, it could be said that Lincoln endured more terrible poverty than did the thousands of slaves he would one day liberate.

It has been said that Lincoln inherited honesty and integrity from his parents. Lincoln once said later in life with moist eyes: "All that I am, or hope to be, I owe to my angel mother." Lincoln was very fortunate to have had two fine mothers. Nancy Hanks, his first, died when he was nearly eleven. It is evident Lincoln's formative years were favorably influenced by her teachings. Sally Bush, his stepmother, proved to be a worthy successor by having a strong personality and high ideals. Lincoln thought her to be a "noble woman who had been a good and kind mother to an orphaned boy."

4

It is a fallacy to believe that poverty promotes dishonesty. This is a load of nonsense promoted by socialist liberals who are merely interested in promoting more involvement of government in private matters. The breakdown of the family at all levels of society, rich or poor, is the leading contributor to all our societal ills. Governmental programs can never solve problems of morality. Education alone can never solve problems of morality. Politcal pundents, politicians, educators, bureaucrats, sociologists, religious dogma of this world, and "New Age" deception of inner divinity cannot bring a spirit of peace and honesty.

Six thousand years of recorded human "civilized" history proves the point.

Lasting peace will never be a reality on this planet until we as a species learn the way to it. The model of learning the difference between right and wrong must be taught. Furthermore, the model of right and wrong must be exemplified by parents and mentors. The question of what is right and what is wrong can be measured by one word. LOVE!

It is not a matter of one's definition of values. When human interaction is taking place, love is either present or it isn't. There is no substitute for a complete family, consisting of both mother and father to raise a child in the way it should go. Following the example set by love, at all levels of society, leads to peace and honesty. Love is a simple concept, but has an infinite number of applications which takes a lifetime to work on.

DILIGENCE: THE LEADING RULE

Lincoln's sense of honor was his brightest armor, ("THE LIVING LINCOLN," page 143) and his tenacious honesty, his sharpest weapon. On July 1, 1850 Lincoln noted that he was not an accomplished lawyer, but his approach to the practice of law was impressive. The following represents the best advice a sincere counselor could offer.

Lincoln believed the leading rule for an attorney or for any profession was diligence. "Leave nothing for tommorrow which can be done today," he believed. His point being: any business at hand today must be completed before moving on to something else. He lived by this rule, he was absorbed by it. So much so, that in one of the most important lawsuits ever to come before the Illinois court, both parties wanted him to represent them. He was widely respected and sought after.

This simple rule of diligence paid handsome dividends for Lincoln both as an attorney, and later as an effective public servant. Is diligence applicable in 1990's? Indeed it is. Ask any executive how he or she feels about a subordinate who undertakes a task and keeps at it until completion. The executive will render a positive evaluation. As a manager at any level of the work structure, being diligent produces results and is noticed.

A good example of diligence concerns the practice of being task oriented. A former boss of mine in management taught me a good lesson. First, he advised that I should make a "to do" list daily. Secondly, in order to accomplish the variety of tasks at hand, only one should be attempted and accomplished before moving on to the next. Third, he advised to never allow a problem to linger. It can only compound itself. Tackle it as soon as possible and pound away at it with tenacity until a resolution is realized. Diligence in any pursuit, is a must for success.

HONEST THINKING

In 1854 slavery was a burning issue concerning the preservation of the Union. Was it right or was it wrong? Could the prevention of future states making the decision whether to be slave or free, destroy the Union? Lincoln questioned the validity concerning the concept of slavery with honest thinking. He likened the degradation of fellow human beings to that of an ant who toiled to drag a crumb to its nest. The ant would furiously defend the fruit of its

6

labor from any robber assailing it. Unfortunately, for the slave, the fruit of his labor was stolen with no avenue of reciprocating justice. Lincoln stated: "...for although volume upon volume is written to prove slavery a very good thing, we never hear of the man who wishes to take the good of it, by being a slave himself." ("THE LIVING LINCOLN") Lincoln's assessment of the overall situation was that most governments have been based on the denial of equal rights of men. He was not shy to honestly speak out for what was right. He believed it was wrong for anyone to assume it was a moral right in the enslaving of one man by another. Hence, his position and opposition to the expansion of slavery. On August 24, 1855 he wrote to his friend Joshua Speed, ...You know I hate slavery. Honest thinking goes a long way in the measuring of a person's integrity.

INCORRUPTIBLE INTEGRITY

Down through the ages, governmental leaders on all levels have found that personal gain was irresistable. For some reason or reasons they always discover a way to justify personal gain in spite of the ethics of the matter. Not so with our beloved "HONEST ABE." Shortly after taking office as President in 1861, President Lincoln received an impressive array of gifts from the King of Siam. These included a sword of costly materials and exquisite workmanship, a photographic likeness of the King and his daughter, and two very impressive elephant tusks. Lincoln sent a letter of thanks to the King of Siam and informed him that his gifts were greatly appreciated. He accepted the gifts not for his own personal treasures, but to accept them in the spirit of his Majesty's desire as tokens of good will toward the American people. Lincoln made it known to the Congress and instructed the placing of the gifts among the government archives. How many of our leaders today, at all levels, would strive to be honest in every situation, regardless of triviality or circumstances?

Based on news reports from all facets of the media, it is unfortunately common knowledge, and often joked about the graft and corruption that permeates all levels of authority in our country presently. Where are the "Lincolns" when we need them most? How can anyone justify graft and taking what is not theirs? Those who abuse power and violate the trust of the people, have their reward. All we can do is pity them. As the old saying goes: "Every dog has its day!"

ADMIT IT WHEN YOU ARE WRONG

Thank God when the war started going right for the Union. A key figure in this change of fate was the fighting General Ulysses S. Grant. Lincoln certainly appreciated Grant's contribution to the war effort, as was evident in his letter to the General dated July 13, 1863. By now, through neccessity, Lincoln had become rather astute in military matters. He was somewhat against Grant concerning the campaign at Vicksburg. His concern was that Grant was making a mistake when he did not follow the river and join General Banks, but instead turned northward, east of the Big Black. After it was all said and done, Lincoln realized Grant was right and he did not hesitate to personally acknowedge that fact and admitted his error in judgement.

Being honest in error far outweighs the duplicity of a cover-up. Another faux pas of many of our leaders today is the willingnes to sweep a problem under the rug rather than admit to it and move on. There is no disgrace concerning imperfection at any level of authority. It is when that simple honesty of owning up to a situation is clouded by a certain haughtiness that often accompanies authority, causes near irrepairable harm to the respectability of the one who committed the infraction.

Admitting when one is wrong to one's subordinates displays a depth of honesty which is engrained in one's character. It must be developed at an early age if possible. This type of thing cannot be taught from a textbook. It is a concept of action which must be explained concerning the depth of its influence, and also witnessed in action by example. Once again, there is no substitute for parental(2) guidance and mentorship at every level, to teach and exemplify the value of doing good. Good means doing good. There can be only one interpretation to the meaning of the word. The application of it is infinite.

THE ART OF EMPATHY

The battle of Gettysburg in July of 1863 was a crushing blow to the Lee's army and the Southern cause. History shows the battle to have been the turning point of the war. The three day engagement imputed thousands of casualties on both sides. It was hot, intense, and mortifying. At one point, the fighting became so intense the combatants resorted to fist fights and throwing rocks at one another.

With Lincoln's growing knowledge of military science, he realized that if the Army of Northern Virginia crossed the Mason-Dixon line, swift and decisive action could destroy Lee's Army. The prospects of such a crushing blow could put an end to a war that was now very costly and unpopular. The battle at Antietam had given the North its first chance at this, however, this advantage did not materialize. Gettysburg was the second chance. Unfortunately, this opportunity was wasted because of the apparent caution of Major General Meade.

Upon learning this, Lincoln was livid. One must understand his frustration concerning this disappointment. A major reason for the war being so lengthy with excruciating devastation, was largely due to the inaction of the Union Generals to aggressively take the war to the rebels. They were constantly outwitted and outfought. In his frustration, Lincoln wrote a letter of reprimand to General Meade. ... You fought and beat the enemy at Gettysburg; and, of course, to say the least, his loss was as great as yours. He retreated; and you did not, as it seemed to me pressingly pursue him... Lee and his army had their backs against the "wall". Ahead of him was a swollen river his army could not cross. Behind him was the Army of the Potomac. It could have been "checkmate" for the North. It was not to be. In spite of this apparent error in judgment Lincoln never sent the letter, why?

Lincoln came to realize the full magnitude of the horror at Gettysburg due to a letter he recieved from General Oliver O. Howard who commanded a corps there. Several days had passed and Lincoln wrote back stating the fact he was initially "mortified" by Meade's caution, but has come to be profoundly grateful for what was done, without criticism for what was not done. Lincoln went on to praise General Meade as a skillful officer and a true man.

What a wonderful principal of management. Yes, it would have been better if Meade had pursued Lee. Lincoln was right with this assessment, but he would have been wrong had he pursued his point of view and issued a severe reprimand for not following orders. Being honest with himself, Lincoln realized he could never fully appreciate what went on those fateful days in early July, 1863. He exercised the art of empathy, and chose the wise course of discretion. Imagine for a moment, had Lincoln gone ahead and fired off that letter of reprimand to Meade. General Meade would have been forced to resign. Not wise for the North's war effort at that time. They could ill afford to lose good generals. More importantly, however, the reprimand would have destroyed a man. With strength of character, Lincoln realized this. By being honest with himself, he was able to extend empathy toward others. Managers at all levels of authority would do well to internalize this example of President Lincoln's leadership.

One does not need to be a military general or a top executive of a multi-national corporation to exercise empathy. The principal Lincoln used in the above example is profound in its context because we all face a similar situation. The art of empathy, putting oneself in another's shoes, applies at home, school, playground, and at work.

PROFESSIONAL ETHICS

One of Lincoln's favorite quips was: ..."A drop of honey will draw more flies than a gallon of gall." In his own uniqueness he possessed the ability to gain one's confidence in stressful situations. An incident of this nature occurred while practicing law in Springfield, IL. ("HONEST ABE," Alonzo Rothschild, page 82-83) Alonzo Rothschild, in his book, "HONEST ABE," writes the following: For Lincoln in court was truth in action. His simple adherence to facts made as vivid an impression on those who heard him as did his intellectual powers, which, were by the way, of no mean order. Lincoln's method of practice was simple and open.

He was able to easily extract facts from unfriendly witnesses. One particular case involved James T. Hoblit, of Lincoln, Illinois. In his own recollection he mentioned how he was a witness to malicious mischief concerning two boys who were overzealous in persuading a bull to exit a corn field. Mr. Hoblit, a young boy at the time, was hesitant and nervous to testify because he was the only witness at the scene. He was determined to reveal as little as possible to the inquiring attorney, Mr. Lincoln.

Mr. Lincoln must have sensed the young boy's reluctance. As soon as Mr. Hoblit revealed his full name, Lincoln became very interested. Turns out that they were related and he asked him questions about family matters. This put Mr. Hoblit very much at ease, and before he realized, all hostility had left him and Lincoln got the whole story.

Lincoln understood human nature. He realized that when it comes to a way of thinking, human beings cannot be driven to do anything. He believed that when the conduct of people was designed to be influenced, persuasion, kind and unassuming persuasion should be adopted. In order to catch a person's heart, he believed the great high road of reason was required, in order to make that person your friend.

As a television talk-show host, I encounter this sort of thing very often. Most of my guests who appear with me on TV are usually very nervous before taping the show. All the encouragement and preparation seems to go out the window when the bright studio lights are turned on, and people see themselves on the television monitor. Public speaking and television cameras are prime ingredients for intimidation. My technique for interviewing on the set of the show is very much like President Lincoln's method was as a trial lawyer. My desired results are achieved by simple, open methods. The idea is to get people feeling relatively comfortable, by making them talk about themselves, and relating this to the facts pertaining to the interview. On numerous occasions I have been complimented on how comfortable and at ease I made people feel during the interview. The secret is this: Extend an honest, sincere, interest to the people of whom you are dealing.

Once this conveyance becomes a connection, cooperation is at hand. Lincoln realized, in order to facilitate cooperation, methods that were simple and open needed to be employed.

THE LOVE OF MONEY?

Abraham Lincoln never had a love for money. He was once quoted defining wealth as being simply a superfluity of what we don't need. ("THE LIVING LINCOLN") Based on the volumes of text produced of his life since his death, nowhere can any evidence remotely suggest that he was motivated by greed. As a businessman he lost money. The opportunity of acquiring land while a surveyor did not interest him. He sought employment merely as a means to an end to earn his daily bread. He was always kind to his friends and seldom charged or undercharged them for his services.

There were instances ("HONEST ABE," Alonzo Rothschild, page 159-160) where Lincoln thought some fees too exorbitant and refunded the undesired portion. One such case occurred when a gentleman by the name of George P. Floyd desired to rent a house. Lincoln was retained to draw up a lease. When the document reached Mr. Floyd, there was no bill accompanying it. So he sent Lincoln twenty-five dollars to compensate for his work. Within a few days Floyd was astonished by the reply and a ten dollar refund: Dear Sir, I have just received yours of the 16th, with check on Flagg & Savage for twenty-five dollars. You must think I am a high-priced man. You are too liberal with your money. Fifteen dollars is enough for the job. I send you a receipt for fifteen dollars, and return to you a ten-dollar bill.—Yours Truly, A. Lincoln ("HONEST ABE," Alonzo Rothschild) There are many more anecdotes that chronicle Lincoln's handling of money. Suffice it to say, he was motivated by compassion and the honest willingness and desire to always do right by people.

In today's world the above kind of behavior is rare indeed. The argument today may be that costs are much higher, such as interest rates and insurance premiums. This is true, however, there still remains no excuse for greed. The attitude of greed and its results are just as viable now as they were at any time in human history. Little seems to change except the circumstances. Greed is predicated on short sighted thinking and living for the moment. Those possessing the character of Lincoln's caliber are more farsighted and continually display a genuine concern for their neighbor.

INHERENT HONESTY

Lincoln made it a practice to serve himself. ("HONEST ABE," Page 176) He really didn't care to have others wait on him. He was self-reliant to the extreme. It was easier for him to get something on his own rather than have it sent for. He would walk to the house from his office to fetch a document, rather than send willing clerks who were at his disposal. If an open fire needed fuel, he would pick up an axe, shed his coat, and vigorously hit the woodpile. Even as President of the United States, Lincoln never lost the notion, to do what was required himself, seemed simpler than to order it done.

His habit of self-reliance annoyed Mrs. Lincoln. He would often open the front door for visitors himself. If that was not bad enough, he would often do this with less than the appropriate attire which conformed with the conventional requirements laid down by authorities on etiquette. In other words, he dressed comfortably.

On one occasion, when Mary Todd Lincoln was lamenting over a breach of social etiquette of a similar kind, a member of her family said: "Mary, if I had a husband with a mind such as yours has, I wouldn't care what he did."

Lincoln was his own wood-sawyer and his own stable-boy. When at home, it was not beneath him to milk the cow or feed the horse. The simplicity and absence of all pretentions carried into his professional life. He hardly ever complained about anything. This mindset, adopted early in his life in the country, allowed him an approach to life to keep things simple. For Lincoln, keeping things simple was chiefly accomplished by employing honesty. He prized honor with modest living above meretricious wealth and the luxuries it might buy. This, however, does not mean that he was stingy or a miser. He was a kind husband and indulgent father. It distressed him to refuse his family anything. All their reasonable wants were cheerfully provided for. In fact his wife once said: "Mr. Lincoln may not be as handsome a figure, but the people are perhaps not aware that his heart is as large as his arms are long." ("HONEST ABE," Page 183) Lincoln was gracious to help others. A typical instance of this was preserved on a slip of paper dated September 25, 1858. It reads:

My old friend Henry Chew, the bearer of this, is in a strait for some furniture to commence housekeeping. If any person will furnish him twenty-five dollars worth, and he does not pay for it by the 1st of January next, I will.

The above example, once again, demonstrates that one does not need to be the greatest President of the United States to display generosity through the motivation of honesty, with a sincere desire to care for others.

CAN'T TAKE IT WITH YOU

When it came to money or other material riches, Lincoln was not impressed with quantity. He was once quoted as saying that if he possessed one hundred thousand dollars, he would consider himself a rich man. The reality, however, was his house in Springfield, and a modest amount of cash. Acquisitions were never a priority for Lincoln. Afterall, what good was it to collect all these goodies if you couldn't take it with you? The standard form of accounting did not yield a surplus of wealth on Lincoln's behalf.

There is another system of accounting, however, which results in quite a different showing. It does not concern dollars and cents, or real estate, nor securities; yet this system of accounting is required to balance the complete picture of the man's assets. Its values are expressed in terms of honor, its profits are to be found in the hearts of the people. He didn't have much to show for a man in his position. Certainly, his colleagues garnered much more, but when it came time for him to meet his destiny, he was presented to a nation as a man that was their ideal of a true man. His reputation was spotless at a time when our country sorely needed such a man. To this day, his name remains a synonym throughout the land for honest dealing. ("HONEST ABE," Page 194)

THE HONEST POLITICIAN?

Honoring the requests of friends, Lincoln began his political career as a candidate for the State Legislature. He had passed numerous little tests of integrity, whereas the people began to trust and confide in him. They loved his kindly nature, laughed at his jokes, applauded his feats of physical strength, and they admired his meager learning because it was employed with so much common sense. The voters desired a member who could be trusted to look loyally, with unsoiled hands, after their material needs at the State Capital. ("HONEST ABE," Page 196) They were looking for good faith as opposed to high ideals. This is a rare commodity in politics today. We as voters and constituents are constantly bombarded with high ideals, which is great, except the high ideals are rarely supported by good faith. They talk the talk, but do not walk the walk.

During the special session of the legislature in 1835-36, Lincoln's sincerity, common sense, and a certain knack for parliamentary work began to be noticed by his colleagues. His favorable notice was chiefly derived by his constant zeal with which he labored. His popularity among the people grew because he was getting things done. They liked him and they trusted him, and even became grateful toward him.

Lincoln had found his niche in life. He loved the arena of politics. The challenges this field of work offered, stimulated his brilliant mind. More importantly, however, it offered him an avenue by which he could help others.

His meager beginnings and chronic states of poverty afforded him the honesty to be a leader who cared enough to change the circumstances which were hurting people. Due to his own financial misfortunes, he endured a lengthy stay in the debtor class. What he endured intensified a natural tenderness for all those suffering a similar fate. It is a well documented fact that Abraham Lincoln was a shrewd politician. This did not detract from his basic honesty. He channeled his energy to serve the best interests of the people, especially to those of whom he represented.

Lincoln's conduct as a politician with regards to a personal rather than a parliamentary point of view, was above reproach. Judge Samuel C. Parks wrote of Lincoln: "I have often said that for a man who was for the quarter of the century both a lawyer and a politician, he was the most honest man I ever knew. ("HONEST ABE," Page 238)

NICE GUYS CAN FINISH FIRST!

Lincoln did not lack for ambition. The same principals that prevented him from taking a shabby case at law, when cases were not too plentiful, held over to keep his politics unsoiled. His ambition was keen, moreso than his need for fees; yet a close study reveals no personal let-down anywhere in his code of honor while following either pursuit. Lincoln could never conceive of the commonly held notion that why there should be one kind of conscience for the private citizen, and a wholly different brand for the politician. Lincoln was a man who experienced prolonged struggles with debt, had a disregard for money, and possessed contempt of those involved in politics to serve corrupt private ends. The key to his success was a fine sense of personal honor. The old saying: "A man usually does best what he likes best to do," is a true and timeless maxim. Lincoln loved politics. His wordly shrewdness was the result of simple honesty. He never mislead himself any more than he did his associates. Lincoln had a penchant for putting himself in the other man's place. This was the reason why he could make so close a calculation as to what another man would do under presumably similar circumstances.

Is it possible for nice people to fair well in this highly competitive world? The answer is yes. The key I believe, lies within Lincoln's philosophy of pursuing success. Please notice, what you the reader are reading and will continue to read in this work, never contains information on how one can intimidate, cajole, or deceive in order to attain success. The key continues to be, and can only be, the presence of an attitude of service toward fellow man.

SEE TO YOUR OWN PUSHING

Few politicians before or since Lincoln possessed the zeal for campaigning with a more spirited assertion. He once wrote to a grumbling politician: "Do you suppose, that I should ever have got into notice if I had waited to be hunted up and pushed forward by older men?" ("HONEST ABE," Page 257) The answer, of course, was no! Lincoln saw to his own pushing, but in an honest way. The following anecdote serves to illustrate an idea of how this was done, concerning a budding politician by the name of John W. Bunn.

"A day or two after my first nomination for city treasurer," writes Mr. Bunn. "I was going uptown and saw Mr. Lincoln ahead of me. 'How are you running?' I told him I didn't know how I was running. Then he said, 'Have you asked anybody to vote for you?' I said I had not. 'Well,' said he, 'if you don't think enough of your success to ask anybody to vote for you, it is probable they will not do it, and that you will not be elected.' I said to him, 'Shall I ask Democrats to vote for me?' He said, 'Yes; ask everybody to vote for you.' Just then a well-known Democrat by the name of Ragsdale was coming up the sidewalk. Lincoln said, 'Now, you drop back there and ask Mr. Ragsdale to vote for you.' I turned and fell in with Mr. Ragsdale, told him of my candidacy, and said I hoped he would support me. To my astonishment, he promised me that he would. Mr. Lincoln walked slowly along and fell in with me again, and said, 'Well, what did Ragsdale say? Will he vote for you?' I said, 'Yes; he told me he would.' "Well, then,' said Lincoln, 'you are sure of two votes at the election, mine and Ragsdale's.' This was my first lesson in practical politics, and I received it from a high source." ("HONEST ABE," page 258) A wonderful first lesson indeed.

There is no essential connection between public life and personal corruption. Or, at least there should not be. Lincoln confuted the common fallacy that there was. The reason there is so much corruption in government today is that many are simply not honest, and are so engrossed in spotless self-love. Doing your own pushing does not mean one must resort to dishonesty to attain a goal. Doing one's own pushing means that one must do his or her part to accomplish something.

That is the primary reason why all the give-away government programs now in force are detrimental to the character building of our nation. We all must learn to pull our own weight and do our own pushing. If one, however, requires genuine help, then so be it. Give-aways or handouts in the long run, breaks down people, it does not help them.

Lincoln was honest with himself. There was always an air of reserve in his demeanor. His modesty helped him to know himself. At times, he was painfully aware of his limitations. He was candid in self-appraisal. He could stand against other men and check off his own shortcomings. Conceit in any form could not be found in him. His freedom of pretention and egotism along with a humble spirit, enabled him to win popular support, disarm criticism and turned aside the darts of envy. His homely fashion helped him to maintain an even keel, regardless of his position in life. The belief that people were not any better or worse than anyone else elevated him to a level of leadership which remains an enigma to those who seek power.

IN A NUTSHELL

Abraham Lincoln was an extraordinary man. As a mere mortal, he was human. He was human in strength as well as weakness. He was not a superhuman, but his composition of character made the brilliance and hardness of a diamond pale in comparison. In a nutshell, Lincoln can best be described as a person of good faith, who was sincere and used common sense. His down-home style enabled him to be liked by most, while his code of honor gained him trust and admiration. He was candid about how he viewed the world and himself. Through his many sufferings he developed a sense of empathy for his fellow man that destroyed the cancer of pretention and conceit.

Ralph Waldo Emerson, who knew Lincoln, described the President's greatness this way: "Abraham Lincoln is perhaps the most remarkable example of this class that we have seen,—a man who was at home and welcome with the humblest, and with a spirit and a practical vein in the times of terror that commanded the admiration of the wisest. His heart was as great as the world, but there was no room in it to hold the memory of a wrong." As the world was beginning to learn of Lincoln's death, Emerson penned the following: "He was the most active and hopeful of men; and his work had not perished: but acclamations of praise for the task he had accomplished burst out into a song of triumph, which even tears for his death cannot keep down."

"The President stood before us as a man of the people. He was thoroughly American, had never crossed the sea...a quite native, aboriginal man, as an acorn from the oak..."

"He offered no shining qualities at the first encounter; he did not offend by superiority. He had a face and manner which disarmed suspicion, which inspired confidence, which confirmed good will." The above description cannot be written of most of us mere mortals. Why is it, the level of honor in Lincoln's character is so rare? Where do we go wrong? These are questions that require a soul searching probe. The implementation of the solution to thse questions cannot be realized in a passive manner. Employing the character trait of honesty requires a proactive state of mind, by which we all look out for each other. The planet Earth is a spaceship racing through the universe. Human kind is its passengers.

Therefore, we are all in the same boat. In this physical existence, there is no better boat. There is no other place to go. Like it or not, we are stuck here together. In the words of a famous utterance: "We must hang together, or we'll hang separately." In order to keep the "boat" afloat, honesty must be the best policy!

Chapter 2
Compassion

FELLOW FEELING IN SUFFERING

Lincoln was a man of many sorrows. He suffered disappointments and setbacks. There are four major trials that rocked Lincoln during the course of his relatively short and tumultuous life. First, was the sudden death of his sweetheart, Ann Rutledge, ("LINCOLN THE UNKNOWN," Dale Carnegie) from which he never fully recovered. Second, was his stormy marriage with Mary Todd. Third, was the early death of two of his sons. Fourth, the rigors of the Civil War.

Any one of the preceding could break a lesser man. Most men would become bitter or commit suicide. Lincoln survived this, but was not unaffected. The wounds ran deep.

William H. Herndon, Lincoln's lifelong friend and law partner described his general state this way:

"If Lincoln ever had a happy day in twenty years, I never knew of it. A perpetual look of sadness was his most prominent feature. Melancholy dripped from him as he walked." ("LINCOLN THE UNKNOWN," Dale Carnegie) From this deep abyss of depression, and a natural affection for the underdog, Lincoln developed a profound sense of compassion rarely equaled before or since.

DEEP SYMPATHY FOR THE SUFFERING

Early on in life, Lincoln developed a deep love for knowledge and thirst for learning. He loved to write his opinions on various topics. His first composition in school was inspired by the cruel sports of his classmates. ("LINCOLN THE UNKNOWN," Dale Carnegie, page 27) They would catch terrapins and put burning coals on their backs. To no avail, Lincoln would plead with them to stop. He ran and kicked off the burning coals with his bare feet. The theme of his first essay was a plea for mercy to animals. He was beginning to show deep sympathy for the suffering which became one of his trademarks.

As was written previously, a true leader cares enough to change the circumstances which are hurting people. In a word, compassion. Compassion does not become manifest through fiat. To truly understand the plight of those who are less fortunate then ourselves, we must have some idea of their situation. It may be derived through personal experience or enough knowledge acquired in order to appreciate the gravity of the situation. Hence, a fellow feeling in suffering must exist.

Lincoln was never a slave per se, however, he did witness the scourge of it. How can a leader of a country, company, group, or family have any idea of one's circumstances, unless a leader can feel for his or her people? How can the abusive husband truly understand the mental and sometimes physical pain he inflicts on his family? Under no circumstances should a leader be a terrorist! How can a man feel for a woman, if he does not know what it is like to be a woman, or visa versa? Anyone who is to be a leader in the same league as Lincoln, must take the time and effort to educate themselves to the point of being highly sensitive to one's needs.

"THE IRON RAN INTO HIM THEN AND THERE"

On his initial trip to New Orleans, Lincoln beheld the true horrors of slavery for the first time.

(LINCOLN THE UNKNOW," Dale Carnegie, page 33-34) He saw negroes in chains and witnessed their being whipped and scourged. He was appalled and was awakened to the realization of what he had read and heard. Later, one of his companions commented on the fact that: "Slavery ran the iron into him then and there." One morning, as they were touring the city, they came upon a slave auction. An energetic and beautiful mulatto girl was being sold like a side of beef. She underwent a thorough examination at the hands of the bidders. The sight of her being pinched and being made to trot up and down the room like a horse repulsed Lincoln. Asking his companions to follow him he said: "By God boys, let's get away from this, If ever I get a chance to hit that thing (meaning slavery), I'll hit it hard. He could not know that one day his developing hatred for man's inhumanity to man would literally place him in position to help save a nation from itself.

"GOD TEMPERS THE WIND TO THE SHORN LAMB" ("THE LIVING LINCOLN," Page 41-42)

In the summer of 1841 Lincoln visited the homestead of his friend, Joshua Speed. On his way back to Springfield, IL he witnessed a sight he would never forget. This event helped to forge a strong feeling of compassion for an oppressed people. In a letter he explained to his friend's younger sister what he experienced.

Lincoln penned that there was a fine example presented on board the boat for contemplating the effect of condition upon human happiness. A gentleman had purchased twelve negroes in Kentucky for the purpose of bringing them back to his farm in the South. They were chained six by six together. They were bound by a small iron clevis around the wrist of each, and this fastened to a main chain. They were strung together as Lincoln put it: like so many fish upon a trot line. ("THE LIVING LINCOLN") He went on to ascertain the fact that this condition was separating these people from the scenes of their childhood, their families, and friends forever! They were headed for a perpetual state of slavery under ruthless masters. In spite of this condition of distressing circumstances, they were the most cheerful and apparently happiest creatures on board. One was playing the fiddle and others sang, danced, told jokes, and played various games of cards. Lincoln surmised the situation with the following: How true it is that "God tempers the wind to the shorn lamb," or in other words, "He tempers the worst of human conditions tolerable, while He permits the best, to be nothing better than tolerable." ("THE LIVING LINCOLN") Isn't it interesting as we examine our own lives how the above quotation rings true. Is anyone ever satisfied with their lot? Most of us are not, until something happens to show us otherwise.

Imagine for a moment your middle class standing, if there's such a thing anymore. Life is okay but it could be better right? The best is nothing better than tolerable. Then, suddenly, something happens to alter your present standing to the worst of human conditions, whatever it may be. You are offered only two choices. One, accept your situation and make the best of it. Or two, rebel and be prepared to fight to the death. The latter sounds more noble, however, it may not be the more expedient. For most of the slaves there simply was no way out. They had no choice, but to accept their lot. They had to make the best out of a bad situation. Doesn't mean they had to like it, but merely accept it and make the best of it. The old addage "turn lemons into lemonade" comes to mind.

Fortunately for us today we need not be concerned, for the moment, about being whisked into slavery. Although we are slaves to this world and everything that goes along with it. The point is there are occasions when we are placed in an untenable situation, with no way out. If we try to make the best of it, by turning lemons to lemonade, being patient, and doing as much as possible to rectify the situation, God will temper the wind to the shorn lamb, and make the worst of our human conditions tolerable.

THEREIN IS A DROP OF HONEY ("THE LIVING LINCOLN," page 49-50)

On February 22, 1842 Lincoln addressed The Washingtonian Society. They sought to reform inebriates through experience of reformed drunkards, quite similar to that of Alcoholics Anonymous today. Lincoln realized that the heavy drinker was a person before he was a problem.

Lincoln sought to compliment the organization for their recent gains in treating drunkards. Lincoln believed the abuse of alcohol to be the greatest evil of all. He, however, realized that people do have weaknesses and can fall prey to disease. His understanding of human nature was uncanny, raising him to towering heights of compassion that would serve him well in the future. He understood that human nature could not be driven to do anything. In the past, treatment required the denunciation of such actions. The old school of thought was harsh denunciation of moral debasements in order to shame the affected soul into repentance. Instead, the opposite prevailed. As Lincoln put it: To have expected them not to meet denunciation with denunciation, crimination with crimination, and anathema with anathema, was to expect the reversal of human nature. ("THE LIVING LINCOLN") In other words, you can't jam it done their throats! Lincoln went on to advise that when the conduct of men is designed to be influenced, persuasion, kind unassuming persuasion, should ever be adopted.

He went on to say that it is an old and true axim: That a "drop of honey catches more flies than a gallon of gall." He advised that if you want to win a man to your cause, first convince him you are his friend. This is where the drop of honey catches his heart. With this bit of compassion and understanding a man would follow the great high road to reason. Lincoln believed and employed the principal of being approachable. Showing a feeling of sympathy and interest in order to persuade. Lincoln also knew very well that lording over people or exercising authority for the mere purpose of being condescending was WRONG! That approach is 100 proof gallon of gall. It is a sad fact in corporate America this sort of thing goes on. Management wonders why there is strife and inefficiency with labor.

It's an age old controversy that goes back to the beginning of time. The spirit born concept of the hierarchy which lends itself to lording over people. It is true there must be some form of structure and a measure of authority to get things done in an orderly and efficient manner. This does not, however, give persons in the position of authority to strip their subordinates of their dignity. Taking the great high road to motivate people to do what is proper is the only sure way to earn respect and efficency from labor. The preceding principal of influencing others for a just cause is as valid today as ever before.

THE CRY OF THE WIDOW AND THE ORPHAN

Lincoln was once asked of what religion he belonged. His reply was rather unexpected, but directly to the point. "When I do good I feel good," he said. "When I do bad I feel bad." There is no question that Lincoln derived his moral ethics and profound spiritual understanding from the Bible. It was, after all, the book of which he learned how to read. As an avid reader of the Bible and a devout student of its teachings, he practiced the admonition that pure religion consists of seeing to the needs of widows and the fatherless.

"The cry of the widow and the orphan," said his secretary, "was always in Lincoln's ear." ("LINCOLN THE UNKNOWN," Dale Carnegie, page 189) Mothers, wives, and sweethearts came before Lincoln daily, pleading and seeking pardons for men who had been condemned to be shot. No matter how exhausted or stressed-out he was, Lincoln always had an ear for them. He usually granted their requests. He could never bear to see a woman cry, especially if she had a baby in her arms. Later in this study, it will become evident that his outpouring of kindness could not and should not be misconstrued as a sign of weakness.

"CATCHEM and CHEATEM"

As an attorney, Lincoln did his utmost to be as fair as possible concerning his fee for services rendered. His own modest estimate of himself, his compassion for clients in distress, and above all his ever present fear of taking dishonest advantage, proved to be the controlling factors. ("HONEST ABE," Alonzo Rothschild, Page 163) On more than one occasion, he refused to accept a full fee even if it were set by law. If he didn't feel that the case or the amount of work involved to resolve the matter justified the expense, he would insist on less. In one particular case, a man was acting as a conservator for a demented sister, who possessed property that amounted to ten thousand dollars, mostly in cash. A certain adventurer who sought to marry the girl took legal action in order to remove the conservator. The conservator retained one of Lincoln's partners on the circuit, a gentleman by the name of Lamon. The agreed sum to block this hostile takeover was $250. By the time the case came before the court, Lincoln's colleague asked him to step in for him. Lincoln won a complete victory for him within twenty minutes. As they stood within the bar, the man paid the sum. Mr. Lincoln who had been looking on when the money was exchanged said to his junior colleague after the client departed:

"What did you charge that man?"

When the amount was stated, he exclaimed: "Lamon, that is all wrong. The service was not worth the sum. Give him back at least half of it."

Lamon protested because the amount had been agreed in advance. Didn't matter to Lincoln. He insisted half the money be refunded, or he would not accept his share of the fee. The embarrassed junior restored half the fee.

This incident was overheard by the judge. He pulled Lincoln aside and rebuked him for charging too little for services rendered. He accused Lincoln of impoverishing the bar, due to his picayune charges of fees.

"That money," said Lincoln, "comes out of the pocket of a poor, demented girl, and I would rather starve than swindle her in this manner."

The honest and compassionate Lincoln was eventually fined for this infraction. Lincoln's sympathy for his colleagues at the bar was strong. They were forgotten, however, when he sat down to write a bill. Continually influenced by these habits of mind, to the very end, his junior partner Lamon stated that Lincoln's position was that their firm should never, with its consent, deserve the reputation enjoyed by those shining lights of the profession—"Catchem and Cheatem."

To most people of his day, and to most people today, Lincoln's honesty was extreme. It is important to note, that he did not have an aversion to making money. He merely desired to be fair about its acquisition. He also maintained an aversion to garnering additional funds or other forms of residual wealth as a result of his position. Many of his contemporaries were quick to take advantage of "inside information" as a benefit of their profession and circumstances in order to make a "fast buck." Lincoln could not bring himself to take advantage of his profession for personal gain. The opportunities for financial gain presented themselves to him as a grocer, postmaster, and surveyor. He never once availed himself of these "perks."

Lincoln's compasssion for others contributed to his chronic state of poverty. Most people with well paying jobs usually squander their money to achieve a state of poverty. Not honest Abe. His aversion to "ripping off" people and refusal to allow money and the acqusition of wealth to become a "god," nearly left him destitute.

In one period of Lincoln's life he gave poverty as a reason for declining an invitation to visit Joshua F. Speed, whom he really wished he could see. This dear friend who was happily married and living in the South, sent repeated messages to which Lincoln finally replied: "I do not think I can come to Kentucky this season. I am so poor, and make so little headway in the world, that I drop back in a month of idleness as much as I gain in a year's sowing. ("HONEST ABE," Page 173) On occasion, he was grimly humorous: "I am so poor, I do not make a shadow when the sun shines." Within a few months of this lugubrious message, he began a family by marrying Mary Todd.

PROCLAMATIONS OF COMPASSION

On March 10, 1863, Lincoln issued a Proclamation offering those who had been absent without leave(AWOL), an opportunity to rectify the situation. They were extended a pardon as long as they reported back to duty by April 1, 1863. They were to report back to their respective regiments, without punishment, except the forfeiture of pay and allowances during their absence. Those who did not report back by the deadline, would then be subject to arrest as deserters and punished as the law provided.

The question is: why did Lincoln pardon deserters? He addresses this question in the Proclamation. It seems that "evil-disposed" and disloyal persons at various places enticed and procured soldiers to desert and make themselves AWOL from their regiments. As a result, this diminished the strength of the armies and prolonged the war.

Lincoln realized that it was not merely a matter of compassion, but a matter of prudence. The Union could ill afford to track down the deserters and have them shot. He needed bodies to carry on the war effort. The key point, however, is that Lincoln realized that many who were absent, found themselves in this state as a result of deception. As a leader, he realized that the strengthening of the war effort was paramount.

Many of his contemporaries and leaders of today would have gone ahead and "cut their noses to spite their face," and have these people shot on sight. They would have been right, but in the long run, they would have been dead wrong. Prudence coupled with compassion is a mark of a great leader. A lesson we all need to take to heart. Exercising one's own rights, does not necessarily promote good leadership.

On March 11, 1865 Lincoln drafted another Proclamation offering a pardon to those who deserted their regiments. In this case he gave them sixty days to return to their outfits. He understood the importance of promoting a national healing. The war was nearing its end. It was apparent, at this point, that the North would prevail and the Union preserved. Would punishment and retribution promote the national healing process and restoration of the Union? Lincoln knew that it would not. What was paramount now, was not the outcome of the war, but its aftermath. With a sixty day grace period, those who were repentent of their deeds would have an opportunity to take part in the healing process. Once again, Lincoln employed wisdom with compassion to promote what was best for the country.

We, as leaders in our own right, must promote what is in the best interest of our people. As a father, he should promote what is in the best interest of his family without hurting others. As a boss at work, the same principal applies. Regardless of the situation, whether a CEO of a corporation, or a bus boy at some pizza joint, we need to nominate ourselves as a committee of one, to promote the best interest of others without hurting anyone. We must try to understand and be sensitive to one's needs. The mark of a leader today (this means you), cares enough to change the circumstances which are hurting people.

Chapter 3
Candor

THE ART OF PLAIN SPEECH

Another notable trait Abraham Lincoln possessed was the art of plain speech. As the saying goes, he pulled no punches. His goal was to convey his thoughts clearly, and to convey his ideas in the simplest, and most effective manner. I believe his candor was rooted in the humble events dominating his early life. He never had much in the way of material possessions. As noted in the first chapter, he possessed little, but believed that as long as he had what was sufficient to survive, that was enough. There were times, however, where enough was not enough, and candor was his only recourse. His straightforwardness and openess of mind were indeed contributing factors guiding him to his greatness as a leader and orator.

EMPATHY AND RESPECT

Lincoln was a thin, bony, and awkward presence of a figure. When he began to speak, his voice would be high-pitched and nasal. As he got into his presentation, the pitch would drop and his voice would carry to the outer limits of thousands. ("THE LIVING LINCOLN," page 243) On October 30, 1858, Lincoln delivered a speech closing out his intense and sometimes, heated campaign against Stephen A. Douglas for the U.S. Senate. He spoke candidly and with eloquence concerning his own motives.

The slavery issue was first and foremost on the political agenda in this period of American history. The country's division on this issue was dangerously widening. Lincoln summed up the nuts and bolts of the slavery question with plain language. Lincoln believed in strict adherence to the Constitution. He believed, however, the South had the legal right to reclaim their fugitives, and Congress had no business interfering with this institution in their states. On the other hand, Lincoln had a moral and ethical problem concerning the institution of slavery and was against it spreading to new territories. He mentioned that he did not have any harsh resentment toward the Southern people because has he put it:

"I have constantly declared, as I really believed, the only difference between them and us, is the difference of circumstances." ("THE LIVING LINCOLN") Lincoln believed that if he were in their shoes he would probably feel the same way they did. This feeling remained with him throughout the war.

The lesson to be learned here is Lincoln's candid regard for other people. It is well documented that he deplored the institution of slavery and the consequences it rendered to those who happened to have skin of color. In spite of this, however, Lincoln understood the Southern Americans of his day were not responsible for its inception. This was an institution introduced by the British in the seventeenth century. Over two-hundred years had passed to where slavery became so entrenched in Southern society, it became a cultural as well as an economic neccessity. He understood human nature well enough to know that if he were in a similar position, he would probably share the same sentiments.

Two points can be made concerning the above example. First, one must have empathy for the other person's circumstances, and respect the other person's point of view.

Everyone has a point of view. The problem occurs when communication breaks down and hostilities of some sort follow. Exercising effective leadership demands that all points of view are known and understood. A leader must make the effort to understand why a person is thinking in a certain manner. The familiar question: "Is the glass half full, or half empty?" illustrates the point. If person A is in a leadership position, and is of the "full" pursuasion, then his or her task is to understand and seek a meeting of the minds with person B who happens to be of the "empty" pursuasion. We as human beings encounter this type of interaction, hundreds of times throughout life. The next time you find yourself having an opposing viewpoint, try an experiment by seeking a meeting of the minds to resolve the situation.

The second point concerning the resolution of opposing viewpoints, concerns candor. This concept has to work both ways in order for difficulties to be resolved. How often do we see this break down in both personal and business relationships? Strife and misunderstanding occur when two opposing points of view clash. It doesn't matter who's right or wrong. The only sure way to resolve the problem and "bury the hatchet," is to get it all out in the open. There may be occasions when an impartial mediator is required to referee the disagreement. The point is, get it out in the open and respect each other's position in order to arrive at some sort of compromise. Lincoln attempted this concerning secession, but failed. Why? One side refused to compromise!

UNRESERVED IN EXPOSING DECEPTIONS

Another example of Lincoln's candor centers around an issue alarmingly similar to the Viet Nam question of the 1960's. Early in his political career, as a first term Congressman, he experienced the worst side of politics. The notorious justification of deception.

The first session of the Thirteenth Congress erupted into a very heated political struggle. President Polk, addressing Congress, blamed the Mexicans for starting the war. A resolution was passed to perpetuate the conflict. In his first major speech before Congress, Lincoln's candor cut to the chase concerning the heart of the problem. He believed it was unnecessary for the President to authorize the sending of troops to Mexico. Lincoln had reason to believe the Mexicans were in no way molesting or menacing the U.S. or its people. The promotion of an armed conflict with our southern neighbors was something for Congrees to approve, and not the President, thereby making this adventure unconstitutional. He believed the principal motivating factor for this act was to divert public attention from the surrender of "Fifty-four, forty, or fight" to Great Britain, on the Oregon boundary question. Some claim it was a matter of imperialism, in order to expand the United States territory. Isn't it interesting that nearly one hundred and twenty years later a similar deception would be foisted on the American people, an adventure which broke the pride of our nation's power.

Lincoln possessed the courage of his convictions. When he discovered a wrong, he sought to right it. This kind of candor required intestinal fortitude commonly know as "guts." It required conviction to be candid and forge ahead to do what is right or proper, knowing full well a significant

36

amount of flak would follow. In this life, the courage of our convictions will be tested. In order to pass the test, we must learn well from Mr. Lincoln. One must have the courage of conviction, and make a stand for what is right. The most effective way to do this, is to convey thoughts with candor.

Today, is no different than the past. A person's courage of conviction is tested daily. As a leader in your own right, should you cave-in and compromise your beliefs? It would all depend on knowing the difference between right and wrong. The point is, we need to know the facts and have the guts to keep the lines of communication candidly open. Very often, this is not easy. Nothing worthwhile is easy to accomplish. Isn't it worth the use of a little candor and understanding to avoid a war?

"THE WORLD HAS NEVER HAD A GOOD DEFINITION OF THE WORD LIBERTY"

The concept of liberty or freedom has often been misconstrued or misapplied. It is fashionable today for this noble concept to be wildly exaggerated in its interpretation. Most of us have been led to believe freedom means that one has the right to freely express themselves, under any circumstances, or do anything they want when they want to. The true intent of liberty as outlined in the U.S. Constitution is not what is being promoted today. What was Lincoln's view on the concept of liberty?

On April 18, 1864 Lincoln was addressing a group named Sanitary Fair, in Baltimore. (THE LIVING LINCOLN," page 602-603) The war had been raging for three years. He was inspired to explore the meaning of a word that was difficult to define. Lincoln focused on diametrically opposed views of liberty at the time. With some the word liberty meant for each man to do as he pleases with himself, and the product of his labor. With others, however, the same word meant for some men to do as they please with other men, and the product of other men's labor. These are two different and incompatible concepts called by the same name. What is

37

really being exposed here is the difference between liberty and tyranny. The following illustration by Lincoln explains it best:

The shepherd drives the wolf from the sheep's throat, for which the sheep thanks the shepherd as the "liberator," while the wolf denounces him for the same act as the destroyer of liberty, especially as the sheep was a black one. Plainly the sheep and the wolf are not agreed upon a definition of the word liberty; and precisely the same difference prevails today among us human creatures, even in the North, and all professing to love liberty.

Clearly, in the above anecdote, the concept of liberty revolved around two points of view concerning slavery. Prior to the emancipation of the slaves in 1863, the controversy was not over the legality of slavery. It was over the morality of this institution and its justification for spreading to new territories. Depending on one's perspective, determined which side of the issue one supported. Has anything changed? Today in 1990's the concept of liberty is still determined by points of view.

In the U.S. today, the institution of slavery no longer exists. This fundamental question concerning every man's right to come and go as he pleases, has been settled. Are we, however, shackled by another form of slavery which continues to persist? Are we so concerned about the freedom of expression, to where its liberal interpretation exceeds the bounds of decency and morality? Recent events bring this to light.

Let's take the issue of flag burning. Person A maintains a deep respect for the nation's flag and what it represents. This person freely displays the flag on his property showing pride and respect for the country. Person B, on the other hand, decides to exercise his freedom of expression, and burns the flag. Both have differing points of view on what liberty is all about. One has a deep respect for his country and what it stands for, the other has total disrespect for what the flag represents, himself and others.

Another example of differing perceptions of liberty concerns the controversial issue of tobacco smoking. A non-smoker will be offended at the discomfort that is caused when a smoker lights up in a confined space, such as a restaurant or at one time, airplanes. Due to the health hazard caused by smoking, lawmakers have taken steps to restrict its use in public places. The non-smoker has the right and freedom to breath fresh, healthy air. The smoker contends that they also have the right to exercise their freedom to smoke if they so desire. Who's right and who's wrong? Let's examine the motivation here.

I believe that both parties concerned have the right to do what they wish as long as one does not infringe upon the other's right. The smoker, however, is wrong in every instance to exercise this right. Why? It is true and one would be right to assert that one should have the freedom to smoke anywhere and anytime, but at whose expense? The health of non-smokers is jeopardized as the result of passive smoking from the pollution caused by smoking. If the smoker doesn't kill your health, he or she will kill your pocket book in the way of exorbitant medical bills and lost productivity on the job.

This assumption is correct, but it is also flawed. Here's why. I smoked for over twenty years and quit in December 1983. As a smoker, I always extended the courtesy of asking a person or persons within my "smoke vicinity" if they would mind if I lit a cigarette. Most of the time, people didn't mind. Occasionally, I would get, "Yes, I do mind." Was I offended? The answer was no. Did I feel my right to smoke was being infringed upon? The answer was again no.

I did have the right to smoke, but did I have the right to make my neighbor uncomfortable? It is a scientific fact that second hand smoke is more dangerous than the act of smoking itself. The tobacco people would argue to the contrary, but that is to be expected. Anyone who argues this is simply ignorant of the facts or just a plain liar. Did

I have the right to endanger the health of a person I usually didn't know? The answer is no. Did I have the right to smoke in a designated smoking area and commit slow suicide? The answer is yes, but that is debatable. Billions of dollars are wasted on medical bills and lost productivity in the workplace as a direct result of smoking. We all have liberties. The question is: Do we have the liberty to exact or infringe on other people's rights by exacting our own. History proves that we do not. The graveyards are full, from what results of humanity's unwillingnes to yield to discretion as being the better part of valor.

SAY WHAT YOU MEAN AND MEAN WHAT YOU SAY

A leader must also be a teacher. There are occasions when a person is faced with an obvious flaw concerning the other person's viewpoint. For example, suppose an employee is constantly bucking your authority. It seems that at every turn there is a problem. The person is slow, and uncooperative. Lincoln faced this problem many times concerning his generals' refusal to act and obey his orders. They didn't respect him because he simply was not liked, and their disdain for his lack of military knowledge became obvious. How did Lincoln handle these situations?

Lincoln was the type of leader who was easy to work for. He was not a taskmaster, but in the same vein, he insisted upon good quality work. He was no push-over. Lincoln handled his lethargic generals with respect and candor. He was quick to cite their strengths first, and candidly proceeded to point out the error of their ways.

It is important to be candid with people because the lack of it can lead to misunderstanding and underestimation. It does no one any good to be kept in the dark about what you are thinking. If the person has the wrong perception or continues in the error of their ways, it then becomes your fault. It is the reponsibility of the leader to take charge and get a handle on the situation. This type of candor applies to all of us. As I mention throughout this book, we are all leaders of some sort during the course of our lives.

One final note on candor. It is extremely important when having the courage to be candid with someone, to be explicitly clear in conveying ideas. Leave no room for miscommunication or misunderstanding. Say what you mean and mean what you say. Be absolutely certain that you are understood. It may be tedious at times, but it is worth it to have the meaning of what you conveyed repeated, in order to insure that there is no misunderstanding. Depending on the situation, be it a formal encounter, get the understanding in writing. As a leader in your own right, there is no substitute for the art of plain speech in order to travel on the great high road of reason.

Chapter 4
Humor

TAKING THE EDGE OFF

It has been said that if one loses their sense of humor, they have lost everything. How wretched a life this would be without appropriate moments of levity. Regardless of the severity of the situation at hand, there always seems to be a place for laughter.

Emerson wrote: A perception of the Comic appears to be an essential element in a fine character...We must learn by laughter, as well as by tears and terrors. President Lincoln was known for his wit and humor throughout his entire life. Much of his humor was a reaction to taking the edge off of a sensitive situation. A friend made a note of his frame of mind. He was told by Lincoln that although he appeared to enjoy life rapturously, he was, nevertheless, the victim of terrible melancholy. When he mingled with others he sought to indulge in fun and hilarity. When by himself, however, he was overcome by mental depression, so much so, he dared not carry a knife with him. The following illustrations serve as excellent examples in retaining a sense of humor in any circumstance, in order to preserve sanity and cope with life's most tenacious challenges.

The Lincoln and Douglas debates of 1858 were intense. In a polital sense, one can say there was very little love lost between Judge Douglas and Mr. Lincoln. In spite of their intense exchanges, there was room for humor. Judge Douglas tried everything to discredit Lincoln as a viable candidate for the U.S. Senate. At the end of one of his speeches he assailed Mr. Lincoln's career. ("THE HUMOROUS MR. LINCOLN," Keith W. Jennison) He mentioned that Lincoln tried everything and always failed. He tried farming and failed, he tried flatboating and failed, he tried school teaching and failed, he sold liquor in a saloon and failed at that, he tried law and failed, and now he was trying politics, and would soon be doomed to his worst failure of all.

Lincoln rose to reply. He came forward and opened by thanking Judge Douglas for a very accurate history he took a lot of trouble to compile. It was all true and Lincoln concurred on every assessment made by the Judge. Lincoln answered his critic with the following zinger: "There is just one thing that Judge Douglas forgot to relate. He says that I sold liquor over a counter. He forgot to tell you that, while I was on one side of the counter, the Judge was always on the other."

It seems that no one could outwit Lincoln. To a great degree, this requires a measure of talent. To think quick on one's feet in the heat of battle requires concentration, talent, and a unique perspective on life. The key to Lincoln's humor, as we shall continue to notice, was his keen sense of making a point with humor, as opposed to strict frivolity.

This is a fine lesson to those of us who wish to utilize humor to offset a verbal affront.

"I WOULD BE HAPPY TO OBLIGE..."

Another example of humor amid the tumultuous events of the Civil War concerned General Ambrose E. Burnside, who was the Commander of the Army of the Potomac. In December 1862, Burnside assaulted Richmond. For two days he sent wave after wave of his troops against an impregnable position. When he finally withdrew, it was at the expense of thirteen thousand of his men. President Lincoln was frustrated, distressed, and mortified over the inability of his generals to take Richmond.

Many people called on Mr. Lincoln daily for a variety of reasons. One day, a man requested issue of a pass from the President for the purpose of travelling to Richmond. "Well," said the President. "I would be happy to oblige, sir, but my passes are not respected. In the last year and a half I have given passes to two hundred and fifty thousand men to go to Richmond, and not one has got there yet."

Notice the humor laced with a little sarcasm. Certainly the situation in Richmond was serious, but Lincoln felt compelled to make a point. Very often, in the midst of frustration, humor is a natural outlet to take the edge off a situation in order to buck-up and continue to cope in the fiery trial.

THE FOLLY OF MISREPRESENTATION

Lincoln made use of humor in order to expose the error of presumption. He spoke of a preacher back in Indiana who was delivering a sermon in a log meeting house in the woods. ("THE HUMOROUS MR. LINCOLN," page 6) The preacher was wearing old-fashoined baggy pantaloons fastened with one button and no suspenders. his shirt was fastened at the neck with one button. The preacher began his sermon in a loud voice saying: " I am the Christ whom I shall represent this day." Right about that time, a little blue lizard ran up one leg of the pantaloons. The preacher continued speaking while slapping his legs. Soon, the lizard got so high, the preacher became desperate and unbuttoned his pants, let them fall, and kicked them aside while continuing with his sermon. By this time the lizard had gotten underneath his shirt and was circling around. The preacher repeated his text:

"I am the Christ whom I shall represent this day." He then loosened the button of his shirt and proceeded to take it off. Sitting in pews, the congregation was stunned with amazement. In a moment of silence, a dignified elderly lady stood up and pointed a finger at the pulpit and shouted at the top of her voice:

"I just want to say, sir, that if you represent Jesus Christ, then I'm done with the Bible."

Another story Lincoln told concerned a Southern Illinois preacher. He asserted that the Saviour was the only perfect man who ever appeared in this world. He also asserted that there was no record in the Bible of there ever being a perfect woman having lived. Suddenly, the preacher was interrupted by a lady in the congregation who stood up and said: "I know a perfect woman, and I've heard about her every day for the last six years."

"Who was she?" the minister asked.

"My husband's first wife," the lady answered.

Lincoln did not care for prepared sermons, or taking the liberty upon oneself the preeminence of Providence. He was a devout student of the Bible, but avoided organized religion because he refused to accept the doctrines of men that did not agree in principal with the Bible.

Another lesson to be learned here, is that the worst thing a leader can do to lose the respect of his people is to alienate them. Making subordinates feel worthless is not conducive to getting the best cooperation or performance out of people.

How often in the business world do managers or executives establish preeminence over their people. The answer,

I am saddened to report, is all too often. With nearly twenty-five years of exposure to the corporate and organizational world, I can verify my assessment through personal experience. Are you really better than the next guy, just because you got promoted? Does that make you superior? Lincoln was a master at exposing the utter foolishness of preeminence.

EXPERIENCE IS THE BEST TEACHER

In regard to an earlier reference, Lincoln utilized humor to emphasize or illustrate a point. As a young man Lincoln and his family moved from Indiana to Illinois. Prior to crossing into Illinois, he spoke of an incident as they came across a small farmhouse full of children. ("THE HUMOROUS MR. LINCOLN," page 9-10) They ranged in age from seventeen years to seventeen months, and all were in tears. The mother of the family was red-headed, red-faced, and was holding a whip in her right hand.

When I first read this, it sort of reminded me of an elementary school Principal I once had the fear of knowing.

It appeared that she had been chastening her brood. The father of the family stood in the doorway, meek-looking, mild-mannered, seemingly awaiting his turn to suffer her wrath. Lincoln who had taken up the peddling of needles, pins, and notions decided to make an attempt at selling her some notions. Lincoln recounted that when the lady saw him approaching the door, she roughly pushed her husband aside and demanded to know Lincoln's business.

"Nothing Madam," he answered. "I merely dropped in as a I came along to see how things were going."

"Well you needn't wait," she said. "There's trouble here and lots of it, but I can manage my own affairs without the help of outsiders. This is just a family row, but I'll teach these brats their places if I have to lick the hide off every one of them. I don't do much talking but I run this house, and don't want no one sneaking around trying to find out how I do it!"

Lincoln later drew on this experience at a Cabinet meeting concerning the interest foreign powers were taking in the War between the States. The President went on to say: "We must let other nations know that we propose to settle our family row in our own way and teach these brats their places if we have to lick the hide off of each and every one of them. And like that old woman, we don't want any sneaking around by other countries who would like to find out how we are going to do it, either. "Now, Seward, you write some diplomatic notes to that effect." ("THE HUMOROUS Mr. LINCOLN")

Experience can be the best teacher especially when it can be drawn upon for a future application. I am sure that Lincoln had no idea when, where, and how he would recall this incident to act as an analogy concerning matters of state. The point is, he effectively rendered the experience, whether good or bad, to good use.

A BELOVED STORYTELLER

In writing about Lincoln's sense of humor, Herndon, his law partner and biographer said: ("THE HUMOROUS Mr. LINCOLN," page 38)

> "In the role of story-teller I regard Mr. Lincoln as without an equal. His power of mimicry and his manner or recital were unique. His countenance and all his features seemed to take part in the performance. As he neared the pitch or point of the story every vestige of seriousness disappeared from his face. His gray eyes sparkled; a smile seemed to gather up, curtain-like, the corners of his mouth; his frame quivered with supressed excitement; and when the rub of the story—as he called it—came, no one's laugh was heartier than his."

NO SUBSTITUTE FOR DOING WHAT YOU WERE CUT OUT FOR

While living in the wilderness, Lincoln revealed that his father taught him how to work, but not to love it. He admitted he never did like work. He preferred to read, tell stories, crack jokes, talk, and laugh—anything but work. These provided pleasantries for him. His proclivities proved to be an escape from the drudgery of work and life itself. This is probably one reason why he was so good at it. Make no mistake, however, Lincoln did not like work, but he sure did a great deal of it and did not possess the luxury of entertaining laziness for too long.

I believe all human beings possess God given talents. Every person who has ever lived is unique. Just as there are no two snow flakes exactly alike, the same holds true for people. Everyone on this planet has something positive to contribute, regardless if one happens to be the lowliest peasant in a third world country or royalty in a major world power.

Imagine the kind of world we would have, if everyone were allowed to maximize his or her potential in whatever they are good at. Vibrant energetic people living a life consisting of happiness and fulfillment. I know, I'm describing a world that does not exist. My father cautioned me about my refusal to accept the world as it is. Fine, his point was well taken. My point, however, is how much better everything would be if everyone on this planet were allowed to do what they were cut out for. Is that so hard? I'm not talking about welfare programs or other futile governmental attempts that spoil people rather than help them. I'm talking about putting people to the plow they know how to push and have them go for it.

Lincoln was a failure at everything he attempted, as Judge Douglas surmised. Basically, that was a correct assessment. Lincoln did not come into his own until he ended up doing what he was cut out for. He became a politician. His only true professional goal in life. Why? Because he liked that sort of work, and it best exploited his God given talents.

I am happiest when I speak publically, and when I am writing. My God given talents are best exploited when I'm doing what I know I've been cut out for. What about you? Are you doing what you like to do? If the answer is negative, then it is time you took steps to change your situation. It is never too late! My public speaking and writing career did not begin until I turned forty-three. To be a "Lincoln" in your own right, put yourself to the plow you love and know how to push, and till the great high road of your life!

SHORT AND SWEET

Lincoln loved the idea of being involved in politics. He had an opinion on just about everything, but when he announced his intentions to run for the Legislature, the people found his manner to be humorous and succinct. "Fellow citizens I presume you all know who I am," Lincoln said. I have been solicited by many to become a candidate for the Legislature. My politics are short and sweet—like the old woman's dance. I am in favor of a national bank. I am in favor of the internal improvement system, and a high protective tariff. These are my sentiments and political principles. If electe d, I shall be thankful; if not it will be all the same." ("THE HUMOROUS MR. LINCOLN," page 12)

Humor is an important component of leadership. It requires a unique skill to bring levity to a serious topic, such as politics. We may all adopt this technique in whatever endeavour we may be engaged. The idea is not to be a"stick in the mud" leader, but one who can inject humor where appropriate. As a leader in any cicumstance, humor can be utilized in order to promote clarity of thought and express one's ideas in utterly simple terms.

ILLUSTRATIONS IN ORDER TO MAKE A POINT

Lincoln told stories in the courtroom in order to illustrate a point for the jury. ("THE HUMOROUS MR. LINCOLN," Page 23-24,27,36,39)

On one particular occasion, he was defending a man against an assult charge. Lincoln thought that it was more like self-defense. He referred to an incident where he once knew a man who was walking down the road with a pitchfork. The man was attacked by a fierce dog. In his trying to ward off the dog, the man impaled the canine with a pitchfork, and killed him. According to Lincoln, the dialogue went as follows:

"What made you kill my dog?" said the farmer.

"What made your dog try to bite me?" the man answered.

"But why didn't you go after him with the other end of your pitchfork?"

"Why didn't he come after me with his other end?"

When I read this anecdote initially, I got quite a chuckle out of it. There is, however, a serious lesson to this. By illustrating the point, Lincoln effectively presented the idea that the end result of an incident, is not what it always appears. Killing a dog with a pitchfork at its first impression appears rather brutal. If the dog, however, was intent on doing harm to the man, the radical defense was justified. Taking the great high road of leadership, demands that one investigates thoroughly, the circumstances of a situation, before rendering a judgement.

Another illustration which bears out a similar point, involves the case of a man who was charged with mistreating a livery horse. A witness testifying for the defendant said, "When his company rides fast, he rides fast; when his company rides slow, he rides slow." The prosecuting attorney then asked how the man rode when he was alone. "I don't know," the witness answered. "I never was with him

Alan Holubesko

when he was alone." In other words, don't ask stupid questions.

In this particular situation, Lincoln was even known to poke fun at his own profession. In a tavern on a bitter winter night, Lincoln joined a group of his fellow lawyers in front of the fireplace.

"Pretty cold night," one man remarked.

"Colder than hell," Lincoln replied.

One of his colleagues turned to him and said, "You've been there, Mr. Lincoln?"

"Oh yes," Lincoln replied. "And the funny thing is that its much like it is here—all the lawyers are nearest the fire."

Lincoln poked fun at his profession. What makes this anecdote humorous is the fact that there is an element of truth involved with the quip. This is a very effective way to make a point.

It should be noted at this juncture, Lincoln was quick with humor, but only used it to illustrate a point. He was a great storyteller, and this was later used against him, by his political opponents. Frederick Trevor Hill, a fellow lawyer, wrote this of Linclon: "In all my experience I never heard Lincoln tell a story for its own sake or simply to raise a laugh. He used stories to illustrate a point, but the idea that he sat around and matched yarns like a commercial traveler is utterly false." Lincoln did nothing in vain. This is a lesson in leadership which cannot be over emphasized.

HOW TO DIFFFUSE A CHALLENGE

In 1846 Lincoln ran for Congress. His opponent was Peter Cartwright, a travelling evangelist with a large following. ("THE HUMOROUS MR. LINCOLN," Page 41) Lincoln was campaigning hard and seemed to have the edge. As with any political race, the opposition brought up everything they could to derail his momentum. He was maligned for being married to a "high-toned Episcopalian," and was accused for not accepting the doctrines of mainstream religion.

Lincoln did try to live by the precepts outlined in the Bible. What he didn't care for were the man-made doctrines and traditions of men, of which most religions are based.

Lincoln attended a religious meeting where Peter Cartwright was preaching. True to form he spoke in a style of exhortation, waving his arms and shouting prayers. Eventually, he calmed down and said, "All who desire to lead a new life, to give their hearts to God and go to Heaven, will stand." A few people, including some men, women, and children rose. Cartwright continued. "All who do not wish to go to hell will stand." Everyone in the meeting hall stood up except Lincoln. Cartwright peered down at Lincoln and said, "I observe that all of you save one indicated that you do not desire to go to hell. The sole exception is Mr. Lincoln, who did not respond to either invitation. May I inquire of you, Mr. Lincoln, where are you going?"

Lincoln rose and spoke quietly. "I came here as a respectful listener. I did not know I was going to be singled out by Brother Cartwright. I believe in treating religious matters with due solemnity. I admit that the questions propounded by Brother Cartwright are of great importance. I do not feel called upon to answer as the rest did. Brother Cartwright asks me directly where I am going. I desire to reply with equal directness. I am going to Congress."

Lincoln won the election by a margin of fifteen-hundred votes. His quick wit and honesty diffused a potentially damaging challenge to his political campaign. There are occasions when taking the great high road of leadership requires quick thinking combined with direct and honest motivations.

POINTED EVALUATION

It was a very well known fact that Lincoln opposed the Mexican War. It was as usual, a political thing. The main issue was the fact that Lincoln and his supporters believed the war was "unnecessarily and unconstitutionally commenced by the President." ("THE HUMOROUS LINCOLN," page 43)

The tact of deterring attention from one controversial matter to another, and the concept of grabbing land and negotiating afterward, is nothing new under the sun. The political concepts which worked very well then, are entrenched in the dawning of twenty-first century politics today.

Lincoln had listended to numerous speeches and utterances forthcoming from the Congress. He commented on the fact that he never saw so many words compressed into so small an idea. He said the whole idea reminded him of a farmer who said, "I ain't greedy for land, all I want is what joins mine." This observation was witty and a bit humorous, but the point was made. America, imperialistic? How can that be? Unrevised history does not lie. Can we as leaders in our own right afford to have the attitude of, what is mine is mine, and what is yours is mine?

As of this writing, we as Americans find ourselves facing a similar diversionary tactic. Should we send our troops to be part of a peacekeeping force in Bosnia? Forget the military quagmire that would ensue, what about the 1.5 billion dollar price tag attached to this adventure? Currently, there is a great political battle being waged on Capitol Hill concerning federal entitlement programs, namely Medicare. If they don't have the money for our own people, where do they propose to come up with billions of dollars to wage war? Well, for those of us who are naive in such matters, suffice it to say that the nonexistent money will be created out of fiat.

What kind of leadership is this? Is this taking the great high road to reason like Lincoln would have? What kind of a model of morality is this sending to our young people? Are you beginning to see the need for this kind of book?

THE "IN" AND "OUT" OF APPEARANCE

Lincoln was conscious of his personal appearance. ("THE HUMOROUS MR. LINCOLN," page 45) He was able to joke about it. Poking fun at himself, he told following story: "One day when I first came to Springfield I got into a fit of musing in my room and stood resting my elbows on the bureau. Looking into the glass, it struck me what an ugly man I was. The fact grew on me and I made up my mind that I must be the ugliest man in the world. It so maddened me that I resolved, should I ever see an uglier, I would shoot him on sight. Not long after this Archie (naming a lawyer present) came to town and the first time I saw him I said to myself, 'There's the man,' I went home, took down my gun, and prowled the streets waiting for him. He soon came along. 'Halt Archie,' said I, pointing the gun at him. 'say your prayers for I am going to shoot you.' 'Why, Mr. Lincoln, what's the matter, what have I done?' 'Well, I made an oath that if I ever saw an uglier man than I am, I'd shoot him on the spot. You are uglier, so make ready to die.' 'Mr. Lincoln, do you really think I am uglier than you?' 'Yes.' 'Well, Mr. Lincoln,' said Archie deliberatley, and looking me squarely in the face, 'if I am any uglier, fire away.'"

It is not disrespectful to say that Lincoln was not outwardly handsome or lacked the aristocratic finesse of his contemporaries. In this respect, he did not take himself seriously. He recognized his limitations. He did not attempt to be what he knew he was not, and poked fun at it. He did not allow his apparent lack of beauty to affect his self-image or detract from his positive view of other people.

It seems, as a result of all the commercial "hype" from Madison Avenue, there is more importance placed on outward appearance than the personal beauty that eminates from within. This philosophy has led to the "me first" kind of thinking, which is the total antithesis of good leadership.

Lincoln was not tidy. His dress could be best described as disheveled. When it came to paperwork, he was a bit lacking. He owned a desk, but most of his paperwork was put into the real working file, his tall silk hat. Lincoln once said of a letter to a fellow lawyer that was neglected, "When I receive the letter, I put it my hat, and buying a new one the next day, the old one was set aside, and so the letter was lost sight of for a time."

The top of his desk was usually a bundle of miscellaneous papers with a note on it saying, "When you cannot find it anywhere else, look into this."

The point is, we all have shortcomings. Nobody is perfect. Lincoln was our greatest leader by many respects, but he did possess certain traits that were wanting. Regardless of our shortcomings or limitations, these should never be allowed to debilitate or demoralize. Lincoln, through the use of humor, points out the harshness of life and one's limitations, should not discourage the "can do" attitude we all need to be successful leaders in taking the great high road in whatever we undertake.

"WANTING TO WORK IS SO RARE A MERIT"

It was not uncommon for Lincoln to put in sixteen to eighteen hour workdays. He did not tolerate the slackness he saw around him. For someone who did not learn to love work, he sure did a lot of it.

Many citizenscalled on the President at the White House. A woman came to see him about the prospect of finding work for her sons. The letter signed by the President read as follows: "The lady bearer of this says she has two sons who want to work. Set them to it, if possible. Wanting to work is so rare a merit it should be encouraged ("THE HUMOROUS MR. LINCOLN," page 80)." The value of a good honest day's work is both beneficial for the worker as well as the employer. Ask any employer who is fortunate enough to have people like this on their staff.

There are times, however, when a leader must use discretion when hiring or firing. Lincoln told a fable to illustrate a point in dealing with a job-seeker.

"Well, Sir, it seems like there was once an old king who was going hunting one day with all his courtiers. He soon met a farmer on the road. The farmer told the king it was going to rain. But the king's astrologer didn't think so. About and hour later there came a cloudburst that proved the farmer to be right; so the king cut off the astrologer's head, and sent for the farmer and offered him the vacant office.

"'It ain't me that knows when it's going to rain,' he said, 'It's my jackass. he lays his ears back.'"

"'Then your jackass is hereby appointed court astrologer,' said the king. And afterwards he realized it was the biggest mistake of his life, because every jackass in the country wanted an office."

In spite of the use of humor and his many shortcomings, Lincoln insisted upon excellence. He expected people to put in a fair day of work with results. There was no room for incompetence or lack of quality. During the War Between the States, Lincoln's generals would discover that even the most patient of men had its limits.

WHOSE SHOES DID YOU EXPECT TO SEE ME SHINING?

A gentlman by the name of Charles Sumner, from Boston, and the powerful Chairman of the Foreign Relations Committee, was admitted to the President's bedroom and was astonished to see Mr. Lincoln polishing his own shoes.

"Whose shoes," asked the President, "did you expect to find me blackening, Mr. Sumner?"

In my years of business and organizational experience, I have found that very often when a person is elevated to a position of authority, they forget how to do things for themselves. Why is it, that those who are elected or appointed to positions of service, end up being the most served? Over the years, there have been many scandals exposed in the high offices of governments, business, and so called non-profit organizations which defiles the connotation of the term "servant."

It reminds me of a story concerning the spoiled husband. This man had been a bachelor for some time. He was self-sufficient and independent. His culinary skills were the admiration of all his female friends. He ironed, sewed buttons, did the wash, and cleaned house, as well if not better than the most meticulous of housewives.

One day, he met a fair lass and fell in love. Soon, they were married. He was a busy man, so his wife did the domestic thing and began doing all the cooking and all the cleaning. As the years rolled by, it was required, because of economic factors, the wife take a job. Being away from home it became very difficult to attend to the chores it demanded.

A funny thing happened to the husband. He suffered memory loss when it came to helping out around the house. His culniary skills were lost. He could not remember how to sew or iron or clean house and wash dishes. What happened? Before marriage, the bachelor could work all day and come home and tend to his domicile. He gets married and all of a sudden he can only do half of what he was capable before. The server became the served, thus becoming spoiled and abusing his position of authority.

Husbands or anyone else in a position of authority, are quick to point out their inherent commission cited within the pages of the Bible and behavioral morays of society. They forget, however, to read on and see that the greatest leaders serve all the more and continue to hold their own. The leader of anything should continue to polish his own shoes, and remain the greatest of servants.

NO EXCUSES, LET'S GET THE JOB DONE!

Lincoln was a man of many sorrows and disappointments. Throughout his life, he utilized humor and a bit of sarcasm in order to cope with tumultuous events. The war had gone very badly for the Union initially. This was partially due to General McClellan's constant demands for more men, guns, and horses. It seemed that he was always in need for more of everything. He knew soldiering, and trained the Army well. Problem was, he rarely took the offensive to engage the enemy. In modern day sports language, he was a good coach, but a lousy manager. As a result of this lack of agressiveness, the North was continually outwitted and outfought in the early going.

Lincoln was a patient man, but after weeks of marching and countermarching continued, it stretched the limits of his tolerance by which he incorporated the following humor: ("THE HUMOROUS LINCOLN," page 96) "It seems to me," Mr. Lincoln said one day. "That McClellan has been wandering around and has sort of got lost. He's been hollering for help ever since he went south. Wants somebody to come to his deliverance and get him out of the place he's got into.

"He reminds me of the story of a man out in Illinois who, in company with a number of friends, visited the State Penitentiary. They wandered all through the institution and saw everything, but just about the time to depart, this particular man became separated from his friends and couldn't find his way out."

"He roamed up and down one corridor after another, becoming more desperate all the time, when at last, he came across a convict who was looking out from between the bars of his cell door. Our man hurried up to the prisoner and asked: "'Say, how do you get out of this place?'"

This bit of sarcasm displays the frustration level Lincoln attained, concerning his general. There comes a time in the practice of management, where enough is enough. For a time, Lincoln would deal with incompetence and insubordiantion with sarcastic humor. His way of crying out: "What can I do about this?" Sooner or later, if the message doesn't sink in, disciplinary action is required.

ANOTHER WAY TO "TAKE THE EDGE OFF"

In 1862, the war continued to go badly for the North. Shortly after the battle of Antietam, Lincoln called for a Cabinet meeting. According to Stanton's account of this meeting, ("THE HUMOROUS LINCOLN," page 99-102) Lincoln entered the room reading a small book, which seemed to be amusing him. He was reading a chapter from Artemus Ward with great deliberation. Having finished, he proceeded to laugh heartily. Not a single member joined in.

What the President read was a piece called "High-Handed Outrage at Utica." Mr. Lincoln was a bit perplexed at their failure to see the humor in the story. According to Stanton's account he wrote the following: "'Gentlemen, why don't you laugh? With the fearful strain that is upon me night and day, if I did not laugh I should die, and you need this medicine as much as I do.'"

After this, Stanton wrote, Lincoln reached into his hat and pulled out a small piece of paper. On it, was the rough draft of the Emancipation Proclamation. When this document eventually became law, it change the course of U.S. history forever.

Lincoln understood the benefit of humor and its proper use. Most of his enemies and those who did not understand his motivation, thought his humor to be buffoonery. Being the great leader he was, Lincoln saw the value of "comic relief" in the midst of adversity and monumental decisions confronting our nation. It was not a matter of his being flippant toward a dire situation. Not at all. It was his way of loosening up the boys a little, in order to prepare them for the serious business to follow.

A LITTLE HUMOR SPRINKLED WITH MERCY GOES A LONG WAY

An incident in the crowded anteroom of the President's office was recounted by Congressman John B. Alley. ("THE HUMOROUS MR. LINCOLN, Page 111) As Mr. Alley passed through the room he noticed an old man sitting in the corner, crying bitterly. It was a familiar story. The old man's son had been condemned to be shot, and his congressman was so convinced of the boy's guilt, he refused to intervene. Mr. Alley took the old man to see the President and have him tell his story. Mr. Lincoln was saddened and replied:

"I am sorry to say I can do nothing for you. Listen to this telegram received yesterday from General Butler: 'President Lincoln. I pray you not to interfere with the court-martial of the army. You will destroy all discipline among our soldiers.'"

The old man's hope faded away. The President viewed his stricken face, then he explained.

"By jingo, Butler, or no Butler, here goes." He wrote out a note and gave it to the old man. The note read. "Job Smith is not to be shot until further orders from me. A. Lincoln."

The old man looked at the letter with astonishment. "I thought it was going to be a pardon," he said. "But you might decide to have him shot next week."

The President smiled. "My friend," he said. "I see you are not very well acquainted with me. If your son never looks upon death till further orders come from me to shoot him, he will live to be a great deal older than Methuselah.

Another example concerning the effectiveness of humor and mercy combined, involved a young boy who was enticed into the Confederate Army. He was from Kentucky. He deserted and on his way home was arrested and accused of being a spy. He was sentenced to death by hanging. Mr. Lincoln examined all the evidence carefully and commented the following: "If a man had more than one life, I think a little hanging would not hurt this one, but as a man has only one life I think I'll pardon him."

Lincoln was viewed as being too lenient concerning the pardons he granted. The narrow minded thinking of his generals focused strictly on law and order. Lincoln knew, however, that during war, life was cheap. People would be sentenced and condemned at the drop of a hat. The waging of war was a license to kill.

The maxims of great leadership require one to recognize wrongdoing and keep one step ahead of it. The following incident displays the fruit borne of such leadership.

Thaddeus Stevens, one of Lincoln's old supporters, often criticized him on being to free with handing out pardons. ("THE HUMOROUS MR. LINCOLN," Page 111-112) One day, Stevens brought a mother from his own state of Pennsylvania, to the White House. The lady's son was condemned to die because he was caught sleeping at his post. Lincoln listened to all the details of the story knowing how that many of Stevens' constituents were interested in the case.

"Now Thad," asked the President. "What would you do in this case, if you had happened to be President?"

Stevens was not thrilled of having the proverbial "ball" thrown in his court, however, in view of the extenuating circumstances he would of course pardon him.

Lincoln reached for a piece of paper and wrote on it. He handed it to the lady and said: "Here Madam, is your son's pardon."

Mr. Stevens escorted the grateful woman from the White House. As they were leaving she exclaimed: "I knew it was a lie. I knew it was a lie." "What do you mean?" Mr. Stevens asked. "When I left home yesterday," the woman said. "My neighbors told me that I would find that Mr. Lincoln was an ugly man. It was a lie; he is the handsomest man I ever saw in my life."

Lincoln's magnanimous gestures as a leader of his people were beginning to become widely known. Is it no wonder he became our most beloved President? Did he need to beat people into authoritative submission as per his general's advice? Many more examples can be cited to further prove that mercy combined with a little humor goes a long way in taking the great high road of leadership.

Chapter 5
Humility

A PECULIAR AMBITION

When Lincoln settled in New Salem he discovered an opportunity he had been seeking for years. It was a challenge to conquer his fears and learn to speak in public. ("LINCOLN THE UNKNOWN," Dale Carnegie, page 35)

Back in Indiana he didn't have much of an opportunity at this sort of thing, but now it was different. In New Salem there was an organized "literary society" that met every Saturday night in the dining room of the Rutledge tavern.

He soon learned of his unusual ability to influence other men by his speech. This knowledge developed his courage and self-confidence. In a few months Lincoln lost his job as a grocery clerk. Politics was a seething cauldron of controversy, so Lincoln decided to take advantage of his speaking ability and run for office.

He worked on his address for weeks, with the aid of Mentor Graham, the local school teacher. On March 9, 1832, he delivered his first address in New Salem. Lincoln spoke about internal improvements, the navigation of the Sangamon, better education, and justice. The conclusion of his address contained the characteristic humility that would be his trademark for the remainder of his life.

..."Every man is said to have his peculiar ambition. Whether it be true or not, I can say for one that I have no other so great as that of being truly esteemed of my fellow men, by rendering myself worthy of their esteem. How far I shall succeed in gratifying this ambition, is yet to be developed. I am young and unknown to many of you. I was born and have ever remained in the most humble walks of life." He concluded his speech with this extraordinary statement: "But if the good people in their wisdom shall see fit to keep me in the background, I have been too familiar with disappointments to be very much chagrined. Your friend and fellow citizen. ("THE LIVING LINCOLN")

Lincoln was a man of many sorrows. He was familiar with disappointments. He learned many lessons and achieved a greater degree of humility as a result of setbacks. He came to understand very early in his life, that disappointments and setbacks were not failures, but stepping stones on the learning curve of life.

Today is a different story. Children are being taught to think of themselves first, and build up their self-esteem. The focus of importance is on the self. There's even a magazine with the same namesake. The main problem with this particular brand of philosophy, is that it discourages humility. People are actually being taught to think of themselves as the most special and important person to appear on this earth since sliced bread. How very wrong this is. Why? Because this kind of thinking leads to self gratification at the expense of others. This is not what our founding fathers of the Constitution of the United States had in mind, concerning freedom of expression. Young adults graduate from school and they are under the mistaken impression that the world is eagerly awaiting their arrival. As the reality of insignificance becomes apparent, the humbling process begins.

WHERE IN THE WORLD DID ALL THIS WATER COME FROM?"

Lincoln possessed an inquisitive mind. Being raised in the wilderness he was well aware of the order of things in nature, and often pondered its wonder. En route from a campaign swing through New England, in 1848, Lincoln had the opportunity to visit Niagara Falls. He was amazed by its immensity and display of continuous power. He was awed by the estimated five hundred thousand tons of water, which fell with its full weight, a distance of several hundred feet. He marveled that this water would be evaporated by the heat of the sun, to again return as rainfall and continue the perpetual power supply.

As he gazed upon the falls he reflected on the fact this wonder of nature had been in existence for eons. All throughout human history, and prehistory, the falls never froze, never dried, never slept, and never rested. This realization humbled Lincoln. He believed that all that was encompassing in our world bore a part of the big picture. Still, he wondered: "Where in the world did all this water come from?"

It is very humbling to comprehend, as Lincoln did, the power of nature. We dwarf in our physical surroundings. Yet, our intellect, the awesome design and power of the human brain has no equal in this physical universe. We do possess great power and potential. Harnessing this power, along with its correct application requires a lifetime of cultivation.

THE MATTER OF SELF-EVALUATION ("THE LIVING LINCOLN," page 210

Mr. Lincoln responded to a request sent by Mr. C.U. Schlater who was seeking an autograph. He replied in a manner that may be construed as having a low self-esteem. First, Lincoln apologized for the apparent delay in answering his request because the letter had been mislaid. Mr. Schlater requested a "signature with a sentiment." Lincoln replied: I am not a very sentimental man; and the best sentiment I can think of is, that if you collect the signatures of all persons who are no less distinguished than I, you will have a very undistinguishing mass of names.("THE LIVING LINCOLN)

In June of 1858 Lincoln was asked to supply a sketch of his life for the Dictionary of Congress. He chose to offer the barest essentials concerning his life. Due to the fact that he didn't presume to be any more than a regular guy from Illinois, he was probably unaware of his increasing fame.

In spite of the fact that Lincoln lost his bid for the Senate in 1858, some people saw him as the next Republican candidate for the Presidency. In a letter to the editor of the Rock Island Register, he responded by declining to entertain the notion of him running for the Presidency because he felt unfit for the position, an assessment he reiterated on several occasions. Judging by his character, he displayed genuine modesty, but was also savy enough to know that such a movement was premature. Even by April, 1860 he did not consider himself a viable candidate for President.

Being humble does not connotate being stupid. Many tend to underestimate humility for weakness. Lincoln is a classic example in this area. As we continue to study his life within the context of character building traits, we will see that there are no shortcuts to achieving true success in this life.

THE PRESIDENT ELECT REMAINS UNASSUMING

On February 11, 1861 Mr. Lincoln boarded a train to begin his journey from Springfield to the White House. Ever appreciative, Lincoln thanked the people for their kindness. He noted that without assistance from God he could not succeed, with it, he could not fail. "Trusting in Him, who can go with me, and remain with you and be everywhere for good, let us confidently hope that all will yet be well," he said. He then asked the people to remember him in their prayers, and bid them an affectionate farewell. This display of modesty would not diminish, even unto death.

"THE BEST MAN OF US ALL"

In his autobiographical sketch Lincoln lamented his lack of formal education, but did what he could to make up for the lack. The sum total of his formal education did not amount to one year. He scholared mostly on his own. He studied English grammar, and nearly mastered the six books of Euclid. What he may have lacked in education, he made up with strength of character.

Lincoln was despised by those who sought power for their own gain. Even his closest advisors were his adversaries. William H. Seward, one of his chief rivals, who served on his Cabinet, came to see the simplicity of Lincoln's greatness, and would describe him as "the best man of us all." History certainly concurs with this. It has been written that Lincoln's greatness rests in this triumph, and the triumph itself rests in the character of Lincoln.("THE LIVING LINCOLN," page 391

..."LET NOTHING BE DONE THROUGH SELFISH AMBITION"...

The question arises; why did Lincoln remain humble in spite of the tremendous amount of adversity that was to continually befall him his entire life? The answer is found in a book he studied perpetually, the Bible. It states the following: ...Let nothing be done through selfish ambition or conceit, but in lowliness of mind let each esteem others better than himself...(THE BOOK OF PHILIPPIANS, Chapter 2:3)

Lincoln lived by this maxim. What made him great was his lowliness of mind. He remained small in his own eyes, never to place any more importance on himself than was absolutely required.

Lincoln did not seek the Presidency of the United States for selfish ambition or conceit. He was not interested in placing himself in the "best place" in order to feel superior or lord over people. He was not interested in elevating his social status. Rather than aiming for prestige he truly sought to serve, not to be served. Lincoln never sought to elevate himself. Quite the contrary, he was elevated. As the good book says: ... for everyone who exalts himself, shall be abased, but he who humbles himself, shall be exalted... (THE BOOK OF LUKE, Chapter 18:14)

The lesson for us today, in this vein, is quite simple. We should not rush toward the lure of selfish ambitionor conceit. Whom are we trying to impress? Remember, NOBODY GETS OUT OF HERE ALIVE! We should live each day as if it were our last...because someday we will be right!

Wouldn't this be a better world if we all sought to serve each other? History has painfully proven that the opposite does not work. It requires a lowliness of mind, a humble approach to life. This is not to be miscontrued with weakness or stupidity. Lincoln was as humble as they come, but he never backed down from a fight! We should, as he did, stand up for what is right, strength of character! Rather than aiming for prestige, we need to look for ways to serve each other. Then and only then will the law of reciprocity (what goes around comes around) net favorable returns. Beware of pursuing selfish ambition or conceit, for it is a prescription tragically snaring the unexpecting in a deep pit of emptiness and ultimate disappointment.

Instead, it is more productive to be humble, gentle, patient, understanding, and peaceful. Often, discretion is the better part of valor. Resist being haughty. One needs to be farsighted. It is usually better to give in the short-term, in order to acquire in the long-term. Being characterized with these traits adds a dimension to one's life that cannot be equaled. If one desires to be in the same class as Abraham Lincoln, then one must employ the motivation and character traits that were synonymous to his.

THE TRUE MEANING OF THANKSGIVING

We observe Thanksgiving Day in the United States and Canada as a national holiday. Why do we do this? Is it merely a tradition for families to get together and gorge themselves with an abundance of food to the point of gluttony? Or, is it merely a proposition of gobbling down turkey and watching football games? Is there a more profound purpose for the observance of a special day set aside for thanksgiving? Thanksgiving for what? I believe we as a nation have lost sight of what we should really be thankful. Thankful to whom? Thankfulness requires humility. It is important as a leader to understand the concept of grace, where it comes from, why it is needed, and why thankfulness is important.

Abraham Lincoln was a thankful individual. He appreciated whatever he was given or possessed. Didn't matter how much or how little. He realized that it was more important to be in a state of having what he needed as opposed to what he may have wanted. The following Presidential Proclamations in their entirety, coupled with my editorial comments will make it clear of what Thanksgiving Day is all about, but first, a brief history of this holiday.

The original purpose of a thanksgiving day was to set aside a day to give thanks for the blessings of the year. The original Thanksgiving Day was said to have occurred in the autumn of 1621 when the Pilgrims of Plymouth Colony held a festival to celebrate the harvest. After the crops were gathered, Governor Bradford proclaimed a feast day. The colonists invited friendly Indians and they feasted for three days.

After the American Revolution, President Washington issued a general proclamation for a day of thanks on November 26, 1789. This was done after the setting up of the government under the Constitution.

In 1863 President Lincoln proclaimed the last Thursday in November of that year as Thanksgiving Day. This tradition pretty much continued until 1941 when Congress passed a joint resolution, signed by President Roosevelt on December 26, making the fourth Thursday in November of every year Thanksgiving Day.

It was customary to set aside special days to give thanks. Some, were for the purpose of celebrating military victories or other events connected with the welfare of the nation. Lincoln drafted a number of proclamations during the course of the Civil War. The following Presidential Proclamation was issued on October 3, 1863. Please note carefully, the humble tone of these missives.

By the President of the United States of America, A PROCALAMATION ("Messages and Papers of the Presidents" Vol.VIII P:3373)

> The year that is drawing toward its close has been filled with the blessings of fruitful fields and healthful skies. To these bounties, which are so constantly enjoyed that we are prone to forget the source from which they come, others have been added which are of so extraordinary a nature that they cannot fail to penetrate and often even the heart which is habitually insensible to the ever-watchful providence of Almighty God.
>
> In the midst of a civil war of unequaled magnitude and severity, which has sometimes seemed to foreign states to invite and to provoke their aggression, peace has been preserved with all nations, order has

been maintained, the laws have been respected and obeyed, and harmony has prevailed everywhere, except in the theater of military conflict, while that theater has been greatly contracted by the advancing armies and navies of the Union.

Needful diversions of wealth and of strength from the fields of peaceful industry to the national defense have not arrested the plow, the shuttle, or the ship; the ax has enlarged the borders of our settlements, and the mines, as well of iron and coal as of the precious metals, have yielded even more abundantly than heretofore. Population has steadily increased notwithstanding the waste that has been made in the camp, the siege, and the battlefield, and the country, rejoicing in the consciousness of augmented strength and vigor, is permitted to expect continuance of years with large increase of freedom.

No human counsel hath devised nor hath any mortal hand worked out these great things. They are the gracious gifts of the Most High God, who, while dealing with us in anger for our sins, hath nevertheless remembered mercy.

It has seemed to me fit and proper that they should be solemnly, reverently, and gratefully acknowledge, as with one heart and one voice, by the whole American people. I do therefore invite my fellow-citizens in every part of the United States, and also those who are at sea and those who are sojourning in foreign lands, to set apart and observe the last Thursday of November next as a day of thanksgiving and praise to our benficent Father who dwelleth in the heavens. And I recommend to them that while offering up the ascriptions justly due to Him for such singular deliverances and blessings they do also, with humble penitence for our national perverseness and disobedience, commend to His tender care all those who have become widows, orphans, mourners, or sufferers in the lamentable civil strife in which we are unavoidably engaged, and fervently implore the interposition of the Almighty hand to heal the wounds of the nation and to restore it, as soon as may be consistent with the divine purposes, to the full enjoyment of peace, harmony, tranquillity, and union....

In spite of the terrible toll of death, destruction, and suffering to many, there was a great deal to be thankful for. In spite of the force set in motion to destroy the nation, another force was called upon to preserve it. Lincoln was well aware of the fact that a higher power was responsible for the country's relative good fortune. Throughout history, events have revealed that God the Father, the Creator and Sustainer of this Universe determines the outcome of all wars according to his Divine Will. Lincoln was aware of this, and humbled by it. The following Proclamation was issued October 20, 1864.

By The President of the United States of America. A PROCLAMATION. ("Messages and Papers of the Presidents,"Vol.VIII P:3429)

It has pleased Almighty God to prolong our national life another year, defending us with His guardian care against unfriendly designs from abroad and vouchsafing to us in His mercy many and signal victories over the enemy, who is of our own household. It has also pleased our Heavenly Father to favor as well our citizens in their homes as our soldiers in their camps and our sailors on the rivers and seas with unusual health. He has largely augmented our free posterity throughout all generations... population by emancipation and by immigration, while He has opened to us new sources of wealth and has crowned the labor of our workingmen in every department of industry with abundant rewards. Moreover, He has been pleased to animate and inspire our minds and hearts with fortitude, courage, and resolution sufficient for the great trial of civil war into which we have been brought by our adherence as a nation to the cause of freedom and humanity, and to afford to us reasonable hopes of an ultimate and happy deliverance from all our dangers and afflictions:

Now, therefore, I, Abraham Lincoln, President of the United States, do hereby appoint and set apart the last Thursday in November next as a day which I desire to be observed by all my fellow-citizens, wherever they may be, as a day of thanksgiving and praise to Almighty God, the beneficent Creator and Ruler of the Universe. And I do further recommend to my fellow-citizens aforesaid that on that occasion they do reverently humble themselves in the dust and from thence offer up penitent and fervent prayers and supplications to the Great Disposer of Events for a return of the inestimable blessings of peace, union, and harmony throughout the land which it has pleased Him to assign as a dwelling place for ourselves and for our posterity throughout all generations...

Once again, one can readily surmise the humble tone by which Lincoln communicated these proclamations. With humility and respect he continually recognizes the fact that without God's grace in our lives personally and nationally, there can be no lasting success. Regardless of one's religious faith or lack thereof, a nations's destiny is determined by the one who created it. Man's sad and tumultuous six thousand years of recorded history bears this out. There is a direct cause and effect relationship as to why the U.S. became the greatest nation in history. The solemn warning for us is to wake up and get back on the proper track before it is too late. We are failing as leaders individually and collectively as a nation. Time is running out! It behooves us to put every day and especially Thanksgivng Day in its proper perspective. The next time you sit down to dine and gorge yourself on that wonderful turkey and all the trimmings with mom's homebaked apple pie, remember who really is responsible for your good fortune, and be truly thankful!

FASTING AND PRAYER, A CALL TO ACTION

By The President of the United States of America. A PROCLAMATION ("Messages and papers of the Presidents,"Vol.VIII P:3237

The following Proclamation was was written by President Lincoln on August 12, 1861. He could sense that this was going to be a long war. The flow of events were now out of human control. A student of the Bible, Lincoln knew that in times of dire national emergency, the principal of fasting and prayer was enjoined. Once again, pay particular attention to the humble tone of this missive. Our nation today, would do well to be exposed to such a request from the President.

Whereas a joint committee of both Houses of Congress has waited on the President of the United States and requested him to "recommend a day of public humiliation, prayer, and fasting to be observed by the people of the United States with religious solemnities and the offering of fervent supplications to Almighty God for the safety and welfare of these States, His blessings on their arms, and a speedy restoration of peace;" and

Whereas it is fit and becoming in all people at all times to acknowledge and revere the supreme government of God, to bow in humble submission to His chatisements, to confess and deplore their sins and transgressions in the full conviction that the fear of the Lord is the beginning of wisdom, and to pray with all fervency and contrition for the pardon of their past offences and for a blessing upon their present and prospective action; and

Whereas when our own beloved country, once, by the blessing of God, united, prosperous, and happy, is now afflicted with faction and civil war, it is peculiarly fit for us to recognize the hand of God in this terrible visitation, and in sorrowful remembrance or our own faults and crimes as a nation and as individuals to humble ourselves before Him and to pray for His mercy—to pray that we may be spared further punishment, though most justly deserved; that our arms may be blessed and made effectual for the reestablishment of law, order, and peace throughout the wide extent of our country; and that the inestimable boon of civil and religious liberty, earned under His guidance and blessing by the labors and sufferings of our fathers, may be restored in all its original excellence:

Therefore I, Abraham Lincoln, President of the United States, do appoint the last Thursday in September next as a day of humiliation, prayer, and fasting for all the people of the nation. And I do earnestly recommend to all the people, and especially to all ministers and teachers of religion of all denominations and to all heads of families, to observe and keep that day according to their several creeds and modes of worship in all humility and with all religious solemnity, to the end that the united prayer of the nation may ascend to the Throne of Grace and bring down plentiful blessings upon our country...

Someone may ask the question: So they fasted and prayed, what good did it do them? More lives were lost and more destruction ravaged the land than all of the other wars in our nation's history combined.

There is no easy answer to that question. Who knows what was in the hearts and minds of the people at the time? The answer is that God knows! He had His reasons to allow such a travesty to occur. People were in no mood for compromise or negotiation at the height of the controversy. Lincoln was correct when he called for a national day for fasting and prayer. Whether or not the people took to heart his recommendation, only God knows for sure.

THE PROBLEM:

Please notice in the following proclamation issued by President Lincoln concerning the significance of repentance regarding a nation's destiny.

By The President of the United States of America. A PROCLAMATION.("Messages and Papers of the Presidents,"Vol.VIII P:3365)

> Whereas the Senate of the United States, devoutly recognizing the supreme authority and just government of Almighty God in all affairs of men and of nations, has by a resolution requested the President to designate and set apart a day for national prayer and humiliation; and
> Whereas it is the duty of nations as well as of men to own their dependence upon the overuling power of God, to confess their sins and trangressions in humble sorrow, yet with assured hope that genuine repentance will lead to mercy and pardon, and to recognize the sublime truth, announced in the Holy Scriptures and proven by all history, that those nations only are blessed whose God is the Lord;
> And, insomuch as we know that by His divine law nations, like individuals, are subjected to punishments and chatisements in this world, may we not justly fear that the awful calamity of civil war which now desolates the land may be but a

punishment inflicted upon us for our presumptuous sins, to the needful end of our national reformation as whole people? We have been the recipients of the choicest bounties of Heaven; we have been preserved these many years in peace and prosperity; we have grown in numbers, wealth, and power as no other nation has ever known. But we have forgotten God. We have forgotten the gracious hand which preserved us in peace and multiplied and enriched and strengthened us, and we have vainly imagined, in the deceitfulness of our hearts, that all these blessings were produced by some superior wisdom and virtue of our own. Intoxicated with unbroken success, we have become too self-sufficient to feel the necessity of redeeming and preserving grace, too proud to pray to God that made us.

It behooves us, then, to humble ourselves before the offended Power, to confess our national sins, and to pray for clemency and forgiveness.

Now, therefore, in compliance with the request, and fully concurring in the views of the Senate, I do by this proclamation designate and set apart Thursday, the 30th day of April, 1863, as a day of national humiliation, fasting, and prayer. And I do hereby request all the people to abstain on that day from their ordinary secular pursuits, and to unite at their several places of public worship and their respective homes in keeping the day holy to the Lord and devoted to the humble discharge of the religious duties proper to that solemn occasion.

All this being done in sincerity and truth, let us the rest humbly in the hope authorized by the divine teachings that the united cry of the nation will be heard on high and answered with blessings no less than the pardon of our national sins and the restoration of our now divided and suffering country to its former happy condition of unity and peace...

These are powerful and profound words that are as relevant today, as they were when they were first drafted. As a nation, we have lost sight of the fact that God is the supreme ruler in all the affairs of men and nations. Down through the ages, it has been the proclivity of human kind to continually forget this foundational truth, hence the rise and fall of empires. This book is dedicated to the proposition of taking the great high road. The high road of which we must travel in order to attain true success, is the spiritual trail blazed by God Himself. It does not matter whether one believes this or not, the fact remains, Almighty God is the ruler and sustainer of this universe!

We, as human beings will never attain prefection as long as we dwell in the flesh. Therefore, we are naturally weak and we tend to make mistakes. In God's eyes, many of these mistakes are sins. Sins against who? Against Him! The Holy Bible, which serves as a spiritual and historical record of the nation of Israel demonstrates on many occasions, when the nation forgot God and slipped into sin and idolatry, the nation was punished, and ravaged with hard times and destruction. The most devastating war the United States ever experienced, was brought on as a result of sin! As a nation we sinned against God and each other.

This is an ominous omen for us to heed. Things have been going along too smoothly for too long. We are a spoiled people. As Lincoln noted over one hundred and thirty years ago, we are intoxicated with unbroken success. We indeed, have become too self-sufficient to feel the necessity to truly rely on God. Well, that is all beginning to change, now isn't it? Want proof? Just watch the evening news. The day is rapidly approaching, when we, as a nation, will have to answer for our transgressions.

I am not a "Holy Roller" who's preaching gloom and doom. I am not attempting to convert people to a particular religion or cult or what have you. For me, I view religion in the same manner as Lincoln. When I do good, I feel good.

When I do bad, I feel bad. The puzzling question, however, is what is really good, and what is really bad? Today, in our society, we are being pummeled with concepts that promote the idea that good is bad, and bad is good. Case in point: honesty is a character trait which should be viewed as a good thing. How far does an honest politician get? How many people justify cheating on their taxes? How much of cash income is actually reported to the IRS, or simply pocketed? Even if the government is ripping us off, it does not justify a reciprocating gesture.

As we examine our lives collectively as a nation and individually, we begin to see the cloud of deceit becoming more encompassing in our everyday life. How can we expect to progress as a nation when we are characterized by all sorts of crime such as: domestic violence, child abuse, adultery, fornication, thievery, murder, wholesale abortions, and love waxing cold (hatred). My friends, as the good book says, we are truly living in perilous times. We, as a nation are defying unseen spiritual laws that cannot be circumvented! Oh yes, it is not easy to read or be told how far off the track we have gone. It is not easy to admit that as a nation we are wrong in many ways. Chastisement is on our doorstep. Taking the great high road of success and leadership in our lives requires that we humble ourselves. We must sincerely seek the path that leads to us being right with God. Only by having a contrite spirit, and not the spirit of self-sufficiency, or a deceitful heart containing vain imaginations, can we avoid the destructive path that will lead to our nation becoming without form and void.

THE SOLUTION

The following proclamation issued by President Lincoln, suggests what can be done to arrive at a resolution of the nation's problems. This is exactly what is required of us today, in order to remedy our national ills.

By The President of the United States. A PROCLAMATION.("Messages and Papers of the Presidents,"Vol.VIII P:3422)

Whereas the Senate and House of Representatives at their last session adopted a concurrent resolution, which was approved on the 2d day of July instant and which was in the words following namely:

That the President of the United States be requested to appoint a day of humiliation and prayer by the people of the United states; that he request his constitutional advisers at the head of the Executive Departments to unite with him as Chief Magistrate of the nation, at the city of Washington, and the members of Congress, and all magistrates, all civil, military, and naval officers, all soldiers, sailors, and Marines, with all loyal and the law-abiding people, to convene at their usual places of worship, or wherever they may be, to confess and repent of their maniforld sins; to implore the compassion and forgiveness of the Almighty, that, if consistent with His will, the existing rebellion may be speedily suppressed and the supremacy of the Constitution and laws of the United States may be established throughout all the States; to implore Him, as the Supreme Ruler of the World, not to destroy us as a people, nor suffer us to be destroyed by the hostility or connivance of other nations or by obstinate adhesion to our own counsels, which may be in conflict with His eternal purposes, and to implore Him to enlighten the mind of the nation to know and to do His will, humbly believing that it is in accordance with His will that our place should be maintained as a united people among the family of nations; to implore Him to grant to our armed defenders and the masses of the people that courage, power of resistance, and endurance necessary to secure that result; to implore Him in His infinite goodness to soften the hearts, enlighten the minds, and quciken the consciences of those in rebellion, that they may lay down their arms and speedily return to their allegiance to the United States, that they may not be utterly destroyed, that the effusion of blood may be stayed, and that unity and fraternity may be restored and peace established throughout all our borders:

Now, therefore, I, Abraham Lincoln, President of the United States cordially concurring with the Congress of the United States in the penitential and pious sentiments expressed in the aforesaid resolution and heartily approving of the devotional design and purpose thereof, do hereby appoint the first Thursday of August next to be observed by the people of the United States as a day of national humiliation and prayer...

The solution to most of our nation's problems lies within or willingness to become united with purpose to truly be ONE nation under God. Isn't that what we call for everyday, when the "Pledge of Allegiance" is recited in school and elsewhere? We must be willing to admit where we have gone wrong before it is too late! We are close now! Too late, is when we get to a point where we can no longer distinguish between right and wrong. We are nearly there now, because more and more our society becomes further entrenched in the deceit of good being bad, and bad being good.

As citizens and owners of our country, we must take the great high road of leadership and beg God to forgive us of our individual and national sins! We must ask our Divine Creator to shower us with godly wisdom, in order to get us back on the right track. Without God's help, we are nothing! When a nation's endeavors are absent of reliance on Him, all human efforts are in vain. History has proven this to be a fact on many occasions. This, my friends, is the true meaning of humility and thanksgiving!

Chapter 6
Faith

THE ASSURANCE OF HOPE NOT YET REALIZED

Lincoln was an extremely faithful individual. Not particularly affiliated to any religious denomination, he nevertheless, was religious. He believed in the existence of a Divine Power and Creator. He reflected on God's purpose for mankind quite often.

In the summer of 1862 the Union army was once again battered by the rebel forces at the second battle of Bull Run. Lincoln reflected on this misfortune in a stoic manner. The will of God prevails, he reasoned. God could not be for or against the same thing at the same time. ("THE LIVING LINCOLN," page 499)

He believed that it was entirely possible for God to be working out a purpose below that neither side could fathom. He also thought that God would be the ultimate source of determining the outcome of the War. He did not know what God's will in this matter was, however, Lincoln was confident that God would work out his purpose regardless of human machinations. ...He who made the world still governs it... ("THE LIVING LINCOLN," page 508)

...SOME GREAT GOOD TO FOLLOW...

Lincoln had received a letter of encouragement from Eliza Gurney, ("THE LIVING LINCOLN," page 617) a Quaker widow, stressing that the Almighty would strengthen him to accomplish all his "blessed purposes." He expressed indebtedness for the prayers of the people and of the encouraging his reliance on God.

Lincoln wrote: The purposes of the Almighty are perfect, and must prevail, though we erring mortals may fail to accurately perceive them in advance. His faith that all things would work to the good were reflected in the following: Surely He intends some great good to follow this mighty convulsion, which no mortal could make, and no mortal could stay.

The lesson for us today is this: Be aware of people's circumstances and take the time to offer encouragement. Supporting those in time of need is a faith builder. Faith in the notion that no matter how bad things are now, they will get better.

It requires the strength of character to face one's mortality and come to terms with this prospect. We all know that our physical lives are not eternal. Every human being who has ever lived, from the greatest to the least, all meet the same fate. We know this, but when confronted individually with our own mortality, it is a difficult trial.

How can one's faith be built up after being notified of having a terminal disease, such as cancer? Thousands of people face this challenge daily. What do you tell your friends or relatives, who must play this unfortunate "hand" that's been dealt them? Is there a right thing to say? Is there a wrong thing to say? One thing I know for sure, to say nothing, is the worst thing.

Each case has its own particular circumstances, and must be dealt with accordingly. A bit of wisdom goes a long way here. Offering encouragement and help in any way possible are two ways to comfort the affected individual. For all of us, it is extremely important to know, as Lincoln did, that there is a loving God who is in the process of working things out. It is hard for us as mere mortals to comprehend such things in the heat of the moment, but we must have faith in the fact that God knows the big picture, and that all of this will eventually work out to the good. Faith or the assured hope of something not yet realized, is a key component comprising strength of character, and a clear lane on the great high road of individual leadership.

THE HIGH COMPLIMENT OF RE-ELECTION

Lincoln won re-election with a clear majority. He was greatful to be given a second term in office, but his main concern was that a national election in the midst of a great civil war demonstrated the people's resolve to carry on. He had faith in the fact that God directed the people to the right conclusion. For those who were disappointed or pained by this result; Lincoln derived no satisfaction.

In spite of everything that had gone wrong during his first term, Lincoln knew and possessed faith in what he was doing was the proper course of action. It required a faith to know what was right in the face of extremely persistent adversity. In the early going, nothing seemed to go his way. He had problems with his subordinates, the Union was on the verge of destruction, the war was going badly, and his personal problems offered no respite. He wasn't Superman. The mounting stress took its toll. It wasn't easy, it never is.

We face similar challenges in our lives. Certainly not as grand concerning matters of state, but in our own little worlds, they may as well be. Whether one is a leader or a follower, in times of extended stress, an encouraging gesture can serve as a high compliment in order to fortify one's faith in the struggle to know that it will all work out sooner or later.

"FOOLS RUSH IN WHERE ANGELS FEAR TO TREAD"

Lincoln believed that all men were created equal. Equal in the sense to possess certain rights and pursuits to happiness. At the time of the Missouri Compromise, it was suggested that the inhabitants of a territory had the right toward self-government. Lincoln did not dispute the right of self-government, but dissented at whose expense. Whether to allow slavery or not was not the entire question. The problem was as Lincoln put it: "If the Negro is a man, why then my ancient faith teaches me that all men are created equal, and that there can be no moral right in connection with one's making a slave of another." ("THE LIVING LINCOLN") Why could one man have rights and the other have no rights. It didn't make sense from a moral standpoint.

Lincoln placed faith in what made sense. He objected to the fact that there can be a moral right in the enslaving of one man by another. Has anything really changed today? I think not. Let's examine the relationship between management and labor. Generally speaking, the attitude between the boss and the hired hand is not good. The reverse is also true. In my fifteen years of management experience, I found the attitude of the "boss" mentality to be that of a "lording over" or certain preeminence fixation. Conversely, the laborer generally possesses little respect for authority and is always seeking ways to circumvent it. It is wrong for the employer to mentally and financially enslave people based on the premise of risks taken and wages paid. It is equally wrong for the laborer to cheat the employer out of a fair day's work. In either instance, it is a case of fools rushing in where angels fear to tread. An employer has the right to expect the best from his employees, provided they are treated fairly and allowed to retain their dignity.

"THESE POOR TONGUES" ("THE LIVING LINCOLN," page 281

Lincoln was thin, bony, awkward and stood taller than most men of his time. He had a high-pitched tenor voice which would drop somewhat, as he continued to speak. The resonance of his voice carried to the outer limits of a large crowd.

His words were penetrating and rang true, partly because of his great faith in the Declaration of Independence. The argument concerning slavery continued long and hard during the debates. He believed, but was not entirely certain, there was a tendency of those supporting slavery, to be part of a possible conspiracy to make the institution perpetual and universal in the nation. Conversely, those who did not believe it, fell within the same rule: "He who asserts a thing which he does not know to be true, falsifies as much as he who knowingly tells a falsehood." ("THE LIVING LINCOLN," page 248)

The real issue that is perpetual and continues in all aspects of our lives is the eternal struggle between right and wrong. Lincoln said: "...the two principals that have stood face to face from the beginning of time; and will ever continue to struggle. The one is the common right of humanity and the other the divine right of kings. It is the same principal in whatever shape it develops itself. It is the same spirit that says, you work and toil and earn bread, and I'll eat it." ("THE LIVING LINCOLN," page 281)

No matter in what form it manifests itself, it is the same tyrannical principal. There is no difference today. It is true that the circumstances and the dates change, but the nature of it does not.

The problem which exists today is not only the struggle between right and wrong, but the developing assertion that more people simply do not know the difference. In this age of the "quick fix" and "I want it now attitude," more faith is being placed in technology and false hope as opposed to the proverbial wisdom of faith in absolutes. The debate is sure to rage long after our poor tongues are silenced.

"MY DEAR GEORGE..."

In a letter to George C. Latham, a Springfield boy who attended Phillips Exeter Academy with son, Robert Lincoln, Lincoln offered some faithful advice dealing with an absolute. Lincoln was concerned for this young lad, because a year earlier, his son had failed to pass the Harvard entrance examinations. He consoled the boy not to be discouraged because of his failure to enter Harvard. Lincoln encouraged him to try again. Why? Because at having made the attempt, one must succeed in it. "Must" is the key word, Lincoln advised. He assured him from previous experience that one cannot fail if one resolutely determines that one will not. ("THE LIVING LINCOLN," page 349)

The idea is to try again and overcome the obstacles that initially thwarted the endeavour. In exacting faith and wisdom, Lincoln counseled to the fact that in one's temporary failure, there is no evidence that one may not be better, and a more successful person in the great struggle of life, than many others who have succeeded more easily. If we do not allow the feeling of discouragement to prey upon us, Lincoln counseled, in the end we are all sure to succeed.

Life on this planet, as we draw near to the end of the twentieth century, is becoming increasingly challenging. What will it be like in the twenty first century? Based on the moral condition of human existence, it is a frightful prospect indeed. How can one succeed in this era of permanent job loss caused by the downsizing of multinational companies? There are many other issues which confront our stability, most of which is out of our control. So what can we do in the context of taking the great high road of our lives. The answer is simple, but not quite as simple to implement. It requires the strength of character to NEVER GIVE UP!

"TRUSTING IN HIM" ("THE LIVING LINCOLN," page 375)

On February 11, 1861 Lincoln now President-elect, boarded a train that would carry him to Washington. He addressed his friends for the last time. He thanked them for their kindness and expressed sincere gratitude with a feeling of owing them everything. He spoke of his awaiting task, and without the assistance of that Divine Being, who ever attended him, Lincoln felt he could not succeed. He believed with God's assistance he could not fail as long as he trusted in Him.

For those of you who are atheists, the following passage in this book may be challenging to you. There is a God who created this universe! Whether people choose to believe this fact or not, does not make any difference. The notion that this universe and our existence on this planet was created by fiat, is absolute foolishness. Darwin himself, toward the end of his life, began to have problems with his theory of evolution. Why? Ask yourself a logical question. The theory of evolution suggests the notion that life came from nothing. How can nothing beget life? Did you the reader, come from nothing? No, of course not. Life begets life. Creation demands a creator. The awesome, amazingly beautiful, and complex design of creation demands a designer. The fact that this entire physical creation has a mind of its own is illogical and perpetuates a deception in order to mask the truth!

Logic dictates that there is a Divine power which rules this universe. This Divine power did not create the physical universe and us physical beings out of fiat. Life begets life, and with a purpose. Our parents in an act of love caused the conception of our existence. This makes us their progeny. The origination of pro-creation began with the first human being. Based on the premise that life begets life, then it is logical to arrive at the deduction that we are the progeny of Almighty God. Would it be logical for this most loving parent's purpose to condemn us to automatic failure? I think not.

Lincoln understood with every fiber of his being that God is the ultimate ruler of everything. We were created with free moral agency, and we must make choices in this life. Doesn't it make more sense to choose to involve God in our lives, as opposed to nothing? When certain foundational concepts of our Divine Creator are understood, it is totally illogical not to involve the power of the Creator in our lives.

"...STICK TO YOUR PURPOSE." ("THE LIVING LINCOLN," page 482)

Another occasion of Lincoln offering good faithful advice, was to Cadet Quintin Campbell. A West Point cadet and the son of Mrs. Lincoln's cousin, Ann Todd Campbell, Quintin was feeling very badly about his new situation. Lincoln sympathized for the young fellow and assured him in writing, with certainty, that he would soon feel better if he stuck to his resolution of procuring a military education. On the contrary, if he faltered, and gave up, he would lose the power of keeping any resolution, and regret it for the rest of his life. Lincoln offered the advice because he knew well of what he advised.

There is something to be learned here. For a good part of my early life, I was accused of being a quitter. It seemed as though I wouldn't stick to anything. I attempted to master musical instruments, such as the piano and the trumpet. I soon aborted these endeavours because they required a higher price than I was willing to pay. I was not resolved, I faltered. I began swimming lessons at the YMCA, but I soon backed away from the challenge because of fear. I took up sports in high school, but never really excelled because once again, I was not fully resolved to commit myself. I had a basic dislike for schooling because of painful and traumatic experiences which I suffered as a youngster. As a result, I left a college prep school because I didn't have the resolve or the presence of mind to recognize the value of a formal education. It was not until nearly twenty years later, that I would resume and pursue my formal education. Perhaps my will had been broken early on in life. I struggle with following through my resolutions even now.

In the past twelve years, I have learned to make determinations and stick to them, netting a certain amount of personal triumph. My personal battle is far from over, however, I continue to make strides. Completing this present work will be my greatest accomplishment to date. It requires a resolve in spite of many pitfalls. It requires a feeling I have only known for a short time. Lincoln was 100% correct when he advised to adhere to one's purpose, and soon one would feel as well as one ever did.

There lies in wait a great danger today for all of us, especially our younger members of society. The resolve to do what is right and maintain the patience required to see things through, is rapidly diminishing. Who are the culprits robbing us of the true quality of life everyone deserves? We are the victims of our own intellect. In the constant quest to improve our standard of living in this sad world of ours, we continually forget to work on our own human nature. Stop and think about it. Do we interact with each other better now than in the past? An examination of history tells us the contrary. Is there less violence in the world today, than previously recorded? Is there less greed now than before? Are we growing in the areas of ethics and character development, or are we slipping to a primordial dynamic of interaction? Generally, an honest and open assessment of the nature of human character has not changed significantly to reflect a comparable balance in relation to our material improvements. The point is this: Resolving to stick to a purpose of character development and knowing the difference between right and wrong is of paramount importance. In order for us to survive as a nation and a race as we enter the 21st century, we must look out for each other and maintain the faith that all things will eventually work to the good.

REFLECTION ON THE ASSURED HOPE

Lincoln believed the will of God would prevail. In the great American Civil War, both parties claimed to act in accordance with the will of God. Certainly, one had to be wrong. Lincoln reasoned that God could not be for or against the same thing at the same time. He understood that it was quiet possible that God's purpose could be something different from the purpose of either party. God could have saved or destroyed the Union without a war. Yet the war began. Having begun, God could have given final victory to either side, but ultimately He chose for the Union to prevail. A greater purpose was being worked out that most of us still do not understand. Have you ever wondered why people who pray to the same God are quick to kill in the name of that same God?

I attended a convention in Washington DC where one of the guest speakers was the journalist and former hostage, Terry Anderson. As he spoke of his lengthy ordeal, one of the puzzling happenings concerning his captors, was their constant prayer to a compassionate and loving Allah, their God. Wouldn't it be wonderful if people of all faiths practiced or emulated what their foundational doctrines professed?

FOCUSING ON THE GOOD IN PEOPLE

Lincoln, in his fifty-six years of life on this planet, displayed an uncanny ability to have faith in people, and continually sought for the good in everyone. I was priviledged to have known a person in my life who was similar in this regard.

In the fall of 1981, I fulfilled a pledge I made to my father concerning the taking of the Dale Carnegie Course. Most people believe that the program is an exercise in public speaking. This is partially true. The public speaking portion of the course is mainly a means of learning how to more effectively communicate with others, and put into practice the tools required, in order for us to attain a greater degree of our potential as human beings. The course is not primarily designed to make an orator out of someone, however, the by-products of the program have inspired some to go on and pursue endeavors of oration.

I fell into this category. I "found myself" when I overcame some basic fears and successfully completed the course. It would not have been possible if it were not for an individual who had faith in me, and expressed genuine concern for my welfare.

Jack Brogan was the "Lincoln" in my life. A retired elementary school principal, Jack knew how to work with people. I saw him in action as a Dale Carnegie instructor, and I also was privileged to work with him as an asssociate.

Nearly old enough to be my father, Jack respected and admired me, a relationhip with an elder I had never known. He admired me for who I was, and in turn, I respected and admired him. How do I know? He told me on several occasions, how he admired me. This encouraged and built up my faith in people. I asked him why. His answer was short and to the point: "Because you've been through a lot more in your short life, than anything I've experienced," he said. I was stunned. Someone older than I, who admired me. Wow! What a rush I had. In my generation, we were always degraded because we were spoiled! We had to constantly be reminded how tough our elders had it during the GREAT DEPRESSION of the thirties. I've always appreciated and never denied the pain and suffering my elders experienced during those hard years. Did that mean I had to be continually reminded of that fact, and have it jammed down my throat? I didn't think so. My friend Jack, never did that. He treated me with respect and admired what made me special. I will always remember and admire him for what made him special.

They say that behind every successful man, there is a woman. One more short ancecdote I would like to share with you the reader, concerning Jack Brogan and his lovely wife Pat. She, supported Jack in his effort to expose people from all walks of life to the Dale Carnegie program. She was there to assist in the operation of classroom instruction. She possessed the identical attributes of genuine concern for the Dale Carnegie students that went well beyond what the course offered. My association continued with my new-found friends after I completed the course. I also assisted in the classroom instruction and helped Jack sign up prospective students.

As our working relationship developed, so did our friendship. Regarding a work related situation, something occurred, and at this time I cannot recall the details of the incident, but in my own mind, I believed that I had offended Jack. This bothered me, and I sought to clear the air. I approached him and mentioned that if I had offended him on this particular situation, I was sorry. Jack, in his often pensive stare before answering a question replied: "Alan, you could never offend me." To this day, I am profoundly moved and appreciative of his wonderful reply.

For me, Jack was a good leader. In my dealings with him, he always sought the great high road of leadership. He was not perfect. I understood that, but he had faith in me, and I in him. My only regret is that I wish I had known him longer than I did. Eventually, economic forces took control, and we went our separate ways. I lost touch with him, and did not learn of his death until a month after the fact. I regret not having the opportunity to pay my last respects to Jack and to his wife Pat and their children. Above all, I regret the missed opportunity to tell him how much I really thought of him. Having faith in people is a key component to good leadership. A good leader is also secure in his or her role to build up their subordinates. Jack was not threatened by the talents and ability I possessed. Quite the contrary, he sought to develop them. Jack, as with most of us, was insignificant as a mover and shaker of this world. As a leader, however, he possessed attributes of greatness that made him a "Lincoln" in his own right. This greatness is within everyone's power to achieve.

In closing, concerning the matter of faith, I believe there is an army of Abraham Lincolns in this world. It is a small army, but nevertheless, an army. Unfortunately, for the time being, this army is dormant. There are no "Lincolns" at the head of governments in this world at the present time. Whereas, there should be "Lincoln like" individuals at all levels of government on this planet. For the time being in this sad earth of ours, the deck is stacked against anyone possessing and applying the character traits discussed in this book. The forces that are ruling this world presently, have seen to that.

For now, those of us who would put into practice what is outlined herein, must continue in faith, to resist the tendency of our human nature to elevate the self at the expense of others. Hang tough in doing what is good. Doing good requires farsightedness, because those who do good in the beginning will lose the early rounds, but be of good cheer because in the end, we will WIN!

Chapter 7
Love of Family and Country

Abraham Lincoln loved his family. He had an almost fanatical fondness for his two sons, Tad and Willie. Very often on summer evenings, one could find him playing ball with them, ("THE UNKNOWN LINCOLN," Dale Carnegie, page 144) coat-tails flying behind him as he ran from base to base. He was known to shoot marbles with them all the way from the White House to the War Office. At night he wrestled with his sons on the floor. He would also go behind the White House and play with the boys and their two goats. Both lads kept the White House "jumping." They would organize minstrel shows, drill the servants military style, and running in and out of people and interrupting office seekers. They had very little respect for ceremony as their father had. They dashed in on a Cabinet meeting to inform the President that the cat in the basement gave birth to kittens.

The informality of this "family" house was similar to what occurred one-hundred years later during the Kennedy years. On one occasion, Tad climbed all over his father and finally ended up on Lincoln's shoulder and sat astride his father's neck. This infuriated the stern Salmon P. Chase with good reason on this particular occasion, because Chase was discussing the grave financial situation confronting the country. The informality of the Lincoln White House did not impress the Washington elite, which created an air of awkwardness.

To some, Lincoln may have appeared a bit flippant concerning the informality of life within the White House. He had his reasons for this. First of all, the executive mansion was and still is the people's house. It was wide open to the public in those days. Just about any American citizen could visit with the President, and he was gracious to accommodate. Lincoln did not believe that this place should be regarded as a palace. Secondly, I believe Lincoln wanted to provide as much as possible, a relatively average home environment for his children. It was important for the kids to grow up like their peers. Third, I believe the informality acted as a buffer to control the insanity and pressure of the times and requirements of his job. Unfortunately, tragedy struck when Willie came down with a fever and eventually succumbed. The loss of his son was devastating to both Lincoln and his wife Mary. He was familiar with this kind of grief. Years earlier in New Salem, he bitterly mourned the loss of his sweetheart, Ann Rutledge. Lincoln, was a man of many sorrows, but it never deterred his capacity to love.

ABSENCE MAKES THE HEART GROW FONDER

In April of 1848, Lincoln was serving as a freshman Congressman in the first session of the Thirtieth Congress.

Separation caused him to miss his wife and his boys. In a letter to his wife he wrote about the fact that in this troublesome world, we are never quite satisfied. ("THE LIVING LINCOLN," page 115) When his wife Mary was with him, he felt somewhat hindered in attending to business. The implication here, seems to be that she was getting "into his hair." When she departed for Illinois, he soon realized that nothing but business with no variety in his life, became exceedingly tasteless to him. He began to hate the work at hand, he hated to stay in the room by himself. Life was just not the same. He missed her and the boys, and he wanted them back as soon as possible. In effect, he was lonely.

Isn't it always the way? We're never satisfied with our lot in life. For some, it requires a separation to realize how much we love each other. In this respect, Lincoln was no different than any other person. Being busy and having a lot to do, he found his family to be just simply in the way. Now that they were gone, he began to miss their presence. Most of us fall victim to a similar scenario.

In the vein of living each day to the fullest, as if it were our last, and having consideration for others, shouldn't we make a concerted effort to love our families regardless of the circumstances? Why is it, as the only intellectual beings on this planet, do we need to suffer egregiously in order to attain a higher plane of love? I guess the answer lies within the dark side of human nature.

Unconditional love or unrestricted concern for others does not come naturally. It seems to require an unpleasant experience to learn the lesson. If you really love someone, absence will make the heart grow fonder. The wise person will read this and learn the lesson of separation and take it to heart, thereby avoiding the pitfall of not extending a higher level of love.

LOVE DEMANDS TRUTHFULNESS

Lincoln's love for his extended family was not wanting. He was always concerned for others. There were occasions, however, where "tough love" was required.

Lincoln's stepbrother, John D. Johnston was a shiftless sort. He was a classic drifter and opportunist always seeking ways to avoid work. In November of 1851 Lincoln fired off a letter to his stepbrother. He purposed to wake him up to his sqirming and crawling about from place to place which was doing him and their mother no good. ("THE LIVING LINCOLN," page 146) Lincoln scolded his stepbrother for his idle ways which were depleting the families's land assets. He refused to let his brother sell a certain portion of land so that a bit of income due to rental, would be available for their mother.

Lincoln did not take any pleasure in chastening. He did it in order to get his brother to face the truth. The truth being he was destitute because he idled his time away. Lincoln's advice to his brother was this: "Your thousand pretenses for not getting along better, are all nonsense— they deceive nobody but yourself. Go to work is the only cure for your case." Lincoln did later agree to the prospect of selling this particular piece of property, but on the condition that their mother would receive the proceeds.

Showing concern for others, often requires courage to expose the truth, even if it hurts. This was the case with Lincoln and his stepbrother. He needed to be aphoristic so that there could be no mistake concerning what Lincoln was conveying to his brother.

It is an important lesson for us today, to have the courage to extend love in a pointed fashion when neccessary. It is also important to understand the manner in which "tough love" should be administered. Lincoln explained to his brother that he wasn't writing the letter in unkindness, but in truth. Jamming it down someone's throat in an authoritarian or condescending manner should not be the method or objective. Parents should be firm and stern, but never unkind or arrogant. That goes for all of us, regardless of our situation or station in life.

THE LEGITIMATE OBJECT OF GOVERNMENT

A examination of Lincoln's life and numerous historical chronicles reveal the undying love he had for his country. In July of 1854, he pondered of what government should mean to him as a private citizen. ("THE LIVING LINCOLN," page 155) He believed the legitimate object of government was to do for a community of people, whatever they needed to have done, but could not do, at all, or could not do so well for themselves, in their separate and individual capacities. If the people could individually do for themselves, then the government ought not interfere.

Lincoln believed that the desirable things individuals of a people could not do for themselves fell into two categories: those which have relation to wrongs, and those which do not. The first, is the relation to wrongs, such as crimes, misdemeanors, and non-performance of contracts. The second, encompassed areas without wrong which required combined action such as: public roads, public schools, charities, and the machinery of government itself. From this Lincoln reasoned, it appeared that if all men were just, there still would be some who needed the servives provided by government, though not so much would be in that need. A good concept for us today.

The point of government in Lincoln's mind was to pick up the slack from what individuals could not do for themselves. It seems that the opposite is true today. The object of government has been to serve individuals and communities in everything. The relationship between what ought to be and what really exists—is way out of balance. Isn't it a wonder why our budget deficit is so great? Lincoln was very conscious of fiscal responsibility. More on that later. The point is, government in our country has become too big at every level, to the peril of our nation.

"DUTY OF THE WHOLE PEOPLE..." ("THE LIVING LINCOLN," page 173

Lincoln realized slavery was a national rather than a regional problem. He did not like the concept of involuntary servitude nor did he care for its spread to new territories. How could new territory be put to its best use if slavery were allowed to pollute it? He believed slave states were places for poor white people to remove from, not remove to. The purpose for new free states were to be places for poor people to gravitate in order to better their condition. Lincoln also pointed out that there were constitutional problems with all of this, not to mention morality. He insisted that if there is anything which is the duty of all Americans it was this: never entrust to any hands but their own, the preservation and perpetuity of their own liberties and institutions.

The lesson for us today is very plain. Whenever, as an individual or a group we become selfish or greedy, problems are soon to follow. Slavery is wrong, there is no question about that. The financial barons that ran the South, wanted the spread of slavery for economic reasons. In a word, GREED! Did this mean that the people of the South were evil? As Lincoln pointed out, given the times and circumstances, anyone faced with a similar situation would have probably felt the same way. The point is, whenever we put our agenda above everyone else, or think of number "one" first, as an individual or collectively as a group, we are not loving our country. The immortal words of President John F. Kennedy's inauguaral address are haunting. "Ask not what your country can do for you, but ask what you can do for your country."

"ALL MEN ARE CREATED EQUAL"

Lincoln often quoted the Declaration of Independence citing the declaration that "all men are created equal." He cautioned against the tendency of us kicking out or rejecting one form of authoritarian government, only to be saddled with a King and Lords of our own. ("THE LIVING

LINCOLN," page 205) Lincoln was addressing the fact that the Declaration of Independence was meant to be a progressive improvement in the condition of all men everywhere. The reality, however, seemed to be merely a concept to withdraw our allegiance from the British crown. Everything else remained the same, just a new face was put on.

Unfortunately, since the dawn of civilization, predjudice and racism has characterized the darker side of human nature. As leaders in our own right, how can we take the great high road of leadership when in the minds of men, equality does not exist? Oh sure, we have laws guarding against such infractions. We have laws for just about everything in this country of ours. There is one law that cannot be legislated, that is the law of morality. We are quick to criticize and change governments. We are quick to judge others unfavorably, and what solution do we come up with? The same old thing, but just a different face. Or in the modern venacular: "same ol' thing, just a different day." The key component of the character trait concerning love of country is loving each other by deferring to one another.

"ALL SHOULD HAVE AN EQUAL CHANCE."

At Independence Hall, on the anniversary of Washington's birth, Lincoln uttered a profound address. He revealed that he never had a feeling politically that did not spring from the sentiments embodied in the Declaration of Independence. He pondered over the toils and dangers risked by the officers and army who achieved independence. He often wondered what principal or idea kept the country together for so long. It wasn't merely a matter of separating from the mother country. It was not only the declaration giving liberty alone to this land, but hope to the whole world for all future time. It was the hope contained therein, which would allow all people to have an equal chance at life. Lincoln's feelings for the basis of the Declaration of Independence ran very profoundly in his character.

101

My friends, we need to possess the same feeling and conviction for love of country as President Lincoln. Why? If we don't, we'll simply lose it! As the American Civil War approached its fateful beginning, Lincoln cautioned his dissatisfied fellow countrymen that there was no oath in Heaven to destroy the government, but he would have the solemn one to "preserve, protect and defend" it. We as individual citizens, as leaders in our own right, must preserve, protect and defend what God Almighty has so graciously given us.

Slavery is alive and well today! No, not in the form you may be thinking. Nevertheless, there is a form of servitude rampant in our land today. Most people work entire lifetimes at jobs they absolutely hate or are underpaid for their efforts. In this age of downsizing, many people sacrificed in order to work for a company that promised security in exchange for loyalty. Unfortunately, through corporate greed many are being cut-short just prior to retirement. How sinister, how flagrant, a slap in the face of the working man. What are these displaced workers to do? Learn a new skill at their age? It is not realistic nor fair. If our national and corporate leaders took the great high road of leadership and applied Lincoln-like character in their dealings with people, this sad condition would not exist in our nation presently. One of the greatest resources this country possesses is the experienced worker. Discarding all that experience and wisdom like wadded-up trash, nets nothing but woe for our nation in the future! Leaders of multinational corporations claim that it is a must to tighten the belt in order to remain competitive. This is true now, but who created this situation in the first place? I am not neccessarily in favor of spending billions of dollars on the space program, but the following illustration proves a point.

A friend of mine who was formerly employed as an engineer by a defense contractor who made spacesuits for NASA, shocked me with this revelation; it is highly probable that we cannot put a man on the moon today, because the knowledge and manpower has been downsized. We could do it twenty years ago, but today the knowledge and expertise of the men and woman to get the job done, is fading. This is a somber warning demonstrating that we can downsize ourselves out of existence.

WHAT MADE THIS COUNTRY GREAT

Lincoln possessed a firm grasp on what rested fundamentally in the proper and healthful relationship between labor and capital. ("THE LIVING LINCOLN," page 452-453) He believed that the assumption of labor only being available in connection with capital was false. Another assumption he believed to be false, was whether it was best that capital should hire laborers, thereby inducing them to work by their own consent, or buy them, and drive them to it without their consent. The conclusion derived, was that all laborers were either hired laborers or what was known as slaves. It was further assumed that once one was hired as a laborer, one would be stuck in that position for life. As I wrote previously, a form of slavery still exists today. That servitude is made manifest because the equation has been reversed. Capital gets the higher consideration rather than labor. The basic problem, is that business over the years, simply got too big. What drove them to become too big? GREED!

There is no such relation between labor and capital as assumed. Nor is it true that a free man should be fixed for life as a laborer. Lincoln believed both assumptions to be false, and he was right!

The point is, labor is prior to, and independent of capital. Capital is only the fruit of labor. Capital would not exist if labor did not exist first. Labor is superior to capital and deserves its due consideration. It is true that capital should have its rights, and does.

What made this nation great were the opportunities afforded to those who were willing to WORK! Most of the successful business people in our history started out by providing their own labor which generated capital. As the enterprise grew, the laborer was now able to hire others to help out. Doing this required capital. That capital was the fruit of the first person's labor.

We have had in this country, a just and prosperous system which opened the way to all, giving to all. The by-product of this energy was progress and improvement for everyone. Unfortunately, today we have a condition in our society that curtails the proper relationship between labor and capital. The government is not favorable to those self-starters willing to build an enterprise. I know. I've been self-employed for over ten years. We are being taxed to death.

Most "Ma and Pop" businesses which were the backbone of this nation are a dying breed. The reason: it's getting to costly to stay in business. Everything seems to be geared to the big corporations. The binding fabric of our society was built up on family owned businesses. All that is changing now, to the peril of our nation. "Do-Gooders" in our government have liberally thrown away our wealth by financing a welfare system that hurts people rather than doing its intended purpose of helping those in need. The term "those in need" and its definition is a much debated concept.

GET THE COUNTRY OUT OF DEBT

By the end of 1864 and three years of war, Lincoln faced a national debt of over 1.7 billion dollars. His solution, in part, was for Congress to issue a limited amount of public securities to the nation. The advantage of this, would be that citizens end up being creditors as well as debtors with relation to the public debt. Lincoln percieved that men would not feel much oppressed by a debt they owed to themselves. Our national leaders would do well to read this book and follow Lincoln's lead in all the aspects of leader-ship being discussed. In short, if our leaders took the great high road of leadership, we could eventually get out of the 5 trillion dollar fix we're in now! Unfortunately, this is unlikely because another agenda has emerged which is not in the best interest of the American people.

ACTING IN THE BEST INTERESTS OF ALL

One of Lincoln's greatest qualities as a leader was that of foresightedness. A great deal more on this aspect of Lincoln's character is in the following chapter, dealing with the man's wisdom. I refer to it now because it is appropriate to do so in light of his love of country.

Once the Emancipation Proclamation became a reality, an orderly plan would have to be devised in order to intergrate the former slaves into society. Lincoln proposed three amendments to the Constitution. ("THE LIVING LINCOLN," page 518) First, to provide compensation to every state which would abolish slavery before 1900. Second, to compensate loyal masters whose slaves had been freed by the chances of war. Third, to authorize Congress to appropriate money for colonizing free Afro-Americans with their own consent. Two places under consideration were Haiti and Liberia. In a letter to General Banks on August 5, 1863, Lincoln also proposed that education for young blacks should be included in the plan of reconstruction. The plan never became a reality because its author did not live to implement it.

Lincoln was concerned for all people. If his proposed plan to integrate slaves into freedom had succeeded, I do not believe we would be experiencing the problems our society is confronting at this time. The oppression of slavery has been abolished. The slavery of oppression has not! Lincoln had a viable plan. There were no "hand-outs." He believed that every one should work. Like he advised his step-brother; "if you don't work, you don't eat." Lincoln himself once said of his father: "He taught me how to work, but he didn't teach to love it." Obviously, there were forces in place that had no intentions of allowing the freed slaves a fair chance at life. There's no conspiracy theory suggested here, the facts speak for themselves. Once again, history has shown the breakdown of leadership in human affairs. A true leader will try to change the circumstances that are hurting people. Lincoln epitomized leadership. In November of 1864, Lincoln won re-election by a landslide. ("THE LIVING LINCOLN," page 623)

He won re-election with a majoity of more than 400,000 votes. He carried every state except Kentucky, Delaware and New Jersey, with an electoral vote of 212 to 21. Americans were now beginning to realize the greatness of his leadership. Part of what he wrote in response to his re-election explains it best. "So long as I have been here I have not willingly planted a thorn in any man's bosom." ("THE LIVING LINCOLN," page 624) Sadly, throughout history, we haven't experienced an abundance of this level and high standard of caring for people.

NOTHING LIKE HOME

An old friend of Lincoln's from Springfield paid him a visit. His name was Billy Brown, a storekeeper. The President was so happy to see him. Years later, he spoke of his visit to Lincoln biographer, Ida Tarbell. They spent a wonderful day together talking about the good old days. Trading yarns and just happy to see each other. Lincoln missed home, the rigors of his office were wearing him down, but his overiding love for his country took priority in the following quote: "Billy, you'll never know just what good you've done me. I'm homesick, Billy, just plumb homesick, and it seems as if this war would never be over. Many a night I can see the boys dying on the fields and can hear their mothers crying for them at home, and I can't help it, Billy, I have to send them down there. We've got to save the Union, Billy, we've got to. ("THE LIVING LINCOLN," Page 126)

A true leader possesses a genuine desire to be of service to others. I not talking about "lip service" which seems to be all we're getting today. I'm referring to dedicated service of a person to be a living sacrifice, to the point of total expenditure in order to improve the lot of those served.

Abraham Lincoln was such a leader. You also, can be a "Lincoln" in your own right, if you adopt a similar mindset, and put it into practice in your life. This mindset requires the four letter word, which is love!

PLUCK A THISTLE AND PLANT A FLOWER

Upon notification of Lee's surrender, there was great celebration. In the early years of the war, Lincoln was a "bum." Now that it was finally over, he was a hero. The following day, the President's old friend Joshua Speed was at the White House for a visit. Speed watched as Lincoln granted a request for the release of several draft resisters whose case was presented by two ladies. ("THE HUMOROUS MR. LINCOLN," Page 139) Afterward, when Lincoln and Speed were alone, the President said: "That old lady was no counterfeit. The mother spoke out in all the features of her face. It is more than one can often say that in doing right one has made two people happy in one day. Speed, die when I may, I want it said of me by those who know me best, that I always plucked a thistle and planted a flower where I thought a flower would grow."

Lincoln cared for people. He had no ax to grind when it came to looking out for others. It gave him great pleasure to have the opportunity to make someone's day more pleasant.

MAKE A FRIEND

President Lincoln made it a point to have kind words to say for anybody, that included his enemies. This often brought rebuke from his friends. ("THE HUMOROUS MR. LINCOLN," page 142) One lady asked him how he could speak so kindly of his enemies when he should be seeking ways to destroy them. "But Madam," replied the President. "Do I not destroy them when I make them my friends?"

Lincoln understood the basic concept of Christianity. He was not much for belonging to any religious organization, but he was a Christian. He knew the contents of the Bible.

He also knew what Christ preached; love your enemies. He also knew how to ultimately destroy enemies, the same way Christ did; he made friends out of them.

Lincoln was human and he could not live long enough to make freinds out of all his enemies. No human being can. The point is, we have to keep trying. Making friends out of enemies requires travelling on the highest of the great high road of life.

HONORING FATHER AND MOTHER

Mr. Lincoln loved his parents. He appreciated their love and concern as parents, while he was a youngster. They taught and cared for him to the best of their ability. He learned his lessons well. The time came where they would need his help. His aging parents, after repeated migrations, had taken up their last abode. ("HONEST ABE," Alonzo Rothschild, Page 189) Times were hard, and it seemed that financial embarrassments were on the increase. There were frequent calls for Abraham. How he responded, may be inferred by a letter he wrote to his stepbrother, John D. Johnston: "You already know I desire that neither father nor mother shall be in want of any comfort, either in health or sickness, while they live." Lincoln did not hesitate in his commitment to help and honor his parents.

In this harried world of ours, as we approach the twenty-first century, it seems very easy to forget about our parents. The nursing homes are bursting to capacity, and horror stories of patient abuse surface daily. The nucleus of the family as we once knew it, no longer exists.

People attain a certain age in life and they are put out to pasture. The children say: "We have are own lives to live." To that I say: "BALONEY!!!" The subtlety of wickedness has caused a dangerous flaw in the chain-link fabric of society.

Where were the parents when we were in a state of helplessness? Where were they when we were sick? Where were they when we were to helpless to cloth ourselves, to feed ourselves, and fight our battles? They were there for us

108

when we needed them. So why can't we be there for them when they need us? The geographical separation between parent and child is widening.

Why has this sorry state of affairs been allowed to occur? A major part of the reason is due to the fruits of an age of permissiveness and liberalism. This has led to skyrocketing situations concerning divorce, teen pregnancy, casual drug use, domestic violence, single parenting, premarital sex, venereal disease, and functional illiteracy. What will the nursing homes be like fifty years from now? Will anyone even care about their parents? Maybe not, mainly because most children may not even know who they are in the first place. Will sons and daughters display the depth of caring for their parents as President Lincoln did for his? What good is education, high technology, bigger and better widgets, prosperity, and a higher standard of living, if one's presence concerning strength of character is non-existent? I challenge any doctor, psychologist, educator, politician, "Do-Gooder," or "New-Age Think Tank Guru," to offer an appropriate answer. The time had better arrive, and soon, for our society to once again observe an unchangeable commandment of this universe: HONOR YOUR FATHER AND YOUR MOTHER! The time has come for children to care for their parents in old age, as parents cared for them in their youth. Want to save tax $$$$ on Welfare or any other liberal governmental hand-out?

TAKE CARE OF YOUR OWN!

Is it possible to accomplish what I have claimed in the above assertion. I believe the answer to that question is yes, when and only when the family unit is in tact. Allow me to illustrate the point, with the following example.

As a young boy growing-up in Rhode Island in the early 1950's, I remember a family who lived next door to us who accomplished what I claim. It was a typical family of the period. It consisted of a father, mother, and two children. There was, however, one additional member, the father of the mother. As I recollect, he was in his eighties and confined to a wheelchair. He was quite a character. As little children we would tease him in good fun, and he would chase us around the yard in his wheelchair.

One day, he suffered a severe stroke. Before he died, those of us who used to play with him, visited our infirmed and elderly friend. He lay motionless, cocooned in a plastic oxygen tent attached to his bed. At least one family member stood in vigil. The stroke damage to his brain left him a mere vegetable. As a young lad, I could not understand how he could be concious and not recognize our sheepish salutations. He was not visited in a hospital, but in a bed in his bedroom, at his daughter's domicile. He lived in this state a short while, then died peacefully at home.

The point is this. At one time in our nation's history, we as a people honored our parents. When they got old and sickly, we didn't just farm them off to a nursing home. It is true that one's medical condition can become so complex, that it is impossible to care for such a person at home. Simple common sense dictates that such a condition should be treated in a hospital, or if long-term, a nursing home, as a last resort. It was not that long ago, where most people came into this world at home, and died at home with their families at their bedside both times. How truly sad it is for any human being to die alone in some generic hospital bed, if it is possible to avoid it. What happened to the love we should have for our parents?

In closing, love of family and country requires a proactive mindset of an individual to give of oneself without expecting anything in return. This concept of love toward neighbor is under attack. It is viewed as wrong, when it is right. We are being bombarded with concepts of self-esteem, self-gratification, and winning through intimidation, as the way to attaining fulfillment as a person. How truly diabolical this kind of thinking pollutes a society.

There is no substitute for the outflowing benefit to the giver and the receiver of unconditional love. The best and only way to build up self-esteem, self-gratification, and winning as a result of genuine concern of others, is to practice the universal spiritual law: It is more blessed to give than to receive!

Chapter 8
Wisdom

DISCERNING AND JUDGING CORRECTLY

Abraham Lincoln was a wise man in many respects. The wisdom he acquired has he travelled through life, prepared him for the mission for which he was destined. How did he gain the wisdom required to lead a nation through the most devastating civil war mankind has ever known? How could a man with such a lack of formal education be so educated? He was an intelligent man who lacked education, but did not require education to acquire intelligence. He was a man filled with knowledge and discretion, who possessed understanding and sought wise counsel.

LOFTY TOLERANCE

There is an old proverb that states: A wise man will hear and increase learning.(THE BOOK OF PROVERBS Chapter 1:5)

Lincoln possessed no prejudice against the Southern people. He believed that the people of the North would have felt the same way if the tables were reversed. He did not offer any lofty solutions to the problem, but offered lofty tolerance. As much as he hated slavery, he could empathize with those who did not introduce the institution of slavery, but were stuck with it. After four years of fighting, there was no hatred in Lincoln. He often was quoted as saying: "'Judge not that ye be not judged.' They are just what we would be in their position." ("LINCOLN THE UNKNOWN," Dale Carnegie, page 191)

Was this a "cop out" on Lincoln's part, so that slavery might continue to perpetuate? Quite the contrary, he wanted to destroy the institution, but gradually. The wisdom of proceeding forward slowly is the key here. In a leadership position, one must be quick to empathize with those under their authority. An understanding of another's point of view before rendering a judgement is wise and fruitful. This applies to all who find themselves in a position of leadership such as: husbands, mothers, managers at work, etc.

This wisdom does not happen by fiat. One must acquire understanding through instruction or personal experience, and apply it with an attitude of concern for others. Put yourself in your wife's or husband's shoes. Understand where your subordinates are coming from! They may be totally off the wall, but the point is to let them air their point of view. If they have a point, then be mature enough to admit it. If they are wrong, then be as gentle as possible to guide them in the right direction. Too often in this sad world of ours, we find ourselves "flying off the handle," because we are right and that's all there is to it! It happens too often in business, and much too often in the home. As leaders, we must possess a lofty tolerance and empathize with our families or subordinates before exacting the rigors of authority!

WISDOM IN MAGNANIMITY

Salmon P. Chase, served as Secretary of State on Lincoln's cabinet. To Lincoln's face, he pretended to be his friend. ("LINCOLN THE UNKNOWN," Dale Carnegie page 151-153) When he was out of his sight, however, Chase was the President's ceaseless, bitter, foe. Very often, Chase worked against Lincoln concerning dealings with other people. He would sympathize with those who were offended at the decisions Lincoln frequently had to make, and made the point that if he were running things, they would have been treated fairly. Have you ever experienced someone that was always trying to undermine your authority behind your back? Lincoln was aware of what was going on. "Chase is like a blue-bottle fly," he said. "He lays his eggs in every rotten place he can find."

Lincoln's advisors suggested that he do away with Chase. It got so bad and Chase resented Lincoln's authority so much, he tendered his resignation. The President called his bluff and accepted. Lincoln was annoyed with Chase, but he recognized one thing. "Of all the great men I have ever known, Chase is equal to about one and a half of the best of them." In spite of all the apparent ill feeling between the two, Lincoln performed a wonderful magnanimous act. He conferred the highest honor a President of the U.S. could give; he made him Chief Justice of the United States Supreme Court.

Did Lincoln promote Chase merely to get him out of his hair? Certainly, that was a possibility. I think not in this case, because Chase had tendered his resignation, the perfect opportunity to be done with him. It could have been a clean break, but Lincoln knew that Chase was a very capable and valuable part of the team in spite of the problems. Discretion was the better part of valor. The simple lesson for us today as leaders is this: "One should not cut off their nose to spite their face." An old familiar cliche, but it applies.

THE WISDOM OF MERCY

On April 5, 1864, Lincoln received a letter from a broken-hearted girl. She was very much distressed. She was pregant out of wedlock. Her boyfriend was serving in the Army. She humbly requested mercy in order for her man to acquire a leave of absence so that they could get married and legitimize the relationship. Lincoln was deeply touched by the contents of the communication. He picked up his pen and wrote the following words at the bottom of the letter: "Send him to her by all means."

Lincoln was a master at discretion. He lived by the maxim: "A drop of honey draws more flies than a gallon of gall." He recognized by the repentive tone of the letter, that these kids had suffered enough from their mistake. What would be the point of perpetuating the misery, especially during wartime? He did not need to approve the request. A tyrant would have rejected the plea. Lincoln was a LEADER, he knew that mercy was the best course of action. He empathized with their pain. What was done was done. Prudence dictated the young people be allowed an opportunity to make the best out of the situation. Rendering a "drop of honey" is usually much more difficult, than meating out a "gallon of gall." It is reasonable to assume that it was difficult for Lincoln to do so at times, but mercy for the proper reasons is wisdom in action. Are we to be tyrants or leaders?

THERE'S MORE THAN DIRT IN FARMING

Lincoln realized the potential of agriculture. He believed that regardless of one's extent of education, there was always something to be learned by farming. Every blade of grass was a study. ("THE LIVING LINCOLN," page 299-302)

Getting one's hands dirty, and learning more effective ways to apply the science of agriculture was both profitable and liberating. The fruits of one's labor leading to a bounty of reaping is a wonderful experience. He recognized that thought requires education. Cultivated thought could be best combined with agriculture labor, or any labor based on the principal of thorough work netting the most efficient use with the smallest quantity of ground to each man. Further education could be derived, in the sense of hitting the books to learn better and more efficient ways to farm, by applying the science of agriculture. If people are to busy applying the proper techniques of farming, there would be no time for war. Lincoln believed that no community whose every member possesses this art could ever be victim to oppression in any of its forms. Such communities could be independent of crowned-kings, money-kings, or land-kings. Isn't it interesting since the inception of the Federal Reserve Board, and the Internal Revenue Service in 1913, the money supply has come under stricter control by the few, leading to a greater dependence of government, banking, and gigantic corporations. It is also interesting to note the history of the world since that time.

Prior to 1900, eighty-percent of the Amercian population were farmers, as opposed to twenty-percent being city dwellers. Today, the percentages are reversed. Eighty-percent are city dwellers and twenty-percent are farmers. The reversal continues to expand. We have become dependent on the large and imposing agribusiness run by huge corporations. Most of our food is processed and mainly procured at gigantic supermarkets. Why is it, that the cancer rate prior to 1900 was much lower per capita to the population than present? Could it be processed food? One thing is for sure. Six thousand years of recorded human history reveals that whenever or wherever big business rules the order of the day, it has never been in the best interests of the people.

WISDOM IN PATIENCE

On March 4, 1861, President Lincoln delivered his first Inaugural Address. The nation was moving dangerously closer to civil war. The President counseled patience and judgement over the following question: "Before entering upon so grave a matter as the destruction of our national fabric, with all its benefits, its memories, and its hopes, would it not be wise to ascertain precisely why we do it?" He went on to explain that the Constitution did not protect slavery in the territories. The Union was about to break apart and Lincoln advised caution to know the ramifications of such actions, before it was too late.

I do not believe the American people realized the enormity of the disaster which was about to befall them. How often do we leap before examining every possibility? It is a common human flaw. Unfortunatley, when these decisions affect others, whether it encompasses interaction with each other or on the national scale, the ramifications can be devastating. As leaders in our own right, we must begin to have a certain fear or respect in order to gain knowledge and wisdom. The alternative leads to being a fool, depising wisdom and instruction, driving us to destruction.

"ACT WELL YOUR PART"

During the early going of the Civil War, Lincoln found himself to be lacking in military matters. Remember, his claim to military fame was the Black Hawk War, where his greatest military exploit was the constant battle with mosquitos. He was brushed aside by one his generals when he sought consultation on a military mattter.

Lincoln also discovered the temperment and the mile-long egos that were ever present in men with power. One such case involved Major General David Hunter. ("THE LIVING LINCOLN," page 455) The General became inscensed when he learned that the command in Kentucky had gone to a mere brigadier. He complained to Lincoln stating: "I am

very deeply mortified, humiliated, insulted, and disgraced."
Obviously, he was a disgruntled employee. How did Lincoln
in his wisdom handle this situation?

By return mail, Lincoln fired off a scorching reproof. He
cited the fact that he was well aware of the General's
situation. He assured Hunter that what had been done was
not purposed to dishonor him, but to wake him up! Lincoln
was very blunt and asked him this question: "You constantly speak as being placed in command of only 3,000.
Now tell me, is it not mere impatience? Have you not known
all the while that you are to command four or five times that
many?" Lincoln went on to write assuring the General that
he was sincerely his friend. He stressed that if the General
insisted on continuing to act in this fashion (being a cry
baby), he would be adopting the best possible way to ruin
himself. Lincoln ended his communication with the following admonishment: "Act well your part, there all the honor
lies. He who does something at the head of one regiment,
will eclipse him who does nothing at the head of a hundred."

There are occasions when interacting with others, be it at
home or in the workplace, we tend to feel slighted. A specific
incident which affected me, dates back to 1969. I was in the
Marine Corps serving in Viet Nam at a place called Con
Thien. We were near the DMZ, which was a precarious
place to be at that time. I had been performing my duties
within the command bunker. The opportunity for a mission arose, which was relativley dangerous yet exciting,
given the line of work I was engaged in. I cannot reveal the
nature of my function, because it was and still is classified.

I became miffed when I was not chosen for the assignment. I felt I was the most qualified to accomplish the task
at hand. Besides, I was itching to do something daring. It
was explained to me that because I was the most qualified,
I would be more valuable to stay behind, rather than being
put at risk on this dangerous assignment.

I didn't understand then what I do now. I was being told to act well my part, and there was truly where all the honor did lie! It was better for me to do something with what I had at the time, because it did eclipse the relative nothing I would have encountered had I been chosen for the assignment.

Leadership requires wisdom and good management principals. Honesty and doing what is in the best interest of the subordinate, is the responsibility of the leader. Patience, by putting aside one's personal ego, and having confidence in the leader's judgement, is the responsibility of the subordinate.

BROKEN EGGS CANNOT BE MENDED

It was summer 1862, and the war was continuing to go badly for the North. Lincoln had been accused of having no policy to deal with this situation. He was berated for not officially stating the North's wishes for the restoration of the Union. On the contrary, Lincoln advised his critics to pay closer attention to what he had been saying. Secession had occurred and there was nothing that could be done about eggs that had already been broken. The advice was for the South to come back to the fold before more eggs would be broken. He cautioned the governmnent's enemies who spent the last ten years trying to destroy the Union, that they could not come back into the fold unhurt. The sooner they come back the better, Lincoln reasoned.

The point is this. We must accept responsibility for the ramifications of our actions. Today, too many believe they can mend the eggs they broke. The reality is that it can't happen. The only way to cut down on what is beyond mending, is to refrain from breaking any more eggs. Government waste on all levels needs to stop! The welfare program as we know it, needs to be tossed on the scrap heap! Eggs are being broken daily by the inherent flaws in our system of government. Politicians often refer to the fact that our system of government is far from perfect, but it's the best yet—man has devised. This is probably true, however, what a sad commentary on man's ability to govern himself!

We need to stop breaking the "eggs" in our own lives.

Drug abuse, domestic violence, crime, stealing, adultery, murder, dishonor, lying, coveting, and lack of morality are becoming more pronounced in our foundational fabric as a society. Our nation is now set on a foundation of SAND. If the present trend continues, it's only a matter of time before a strong storm of adversity will sweep us away and break all of our eggs!

EXAMINING THE PROS AND CONS

Concerning the issue of emancipation, Lincoln proceeded slowly. He had no objection on legal or constituional grounds. He was not urging any objections of a moral nature. He viewed the concept as a practical war measure, based on the advantages and disadvantages concerning the suppression of the rebellion. His question was, what possible result of good would follow the issuing of such a proclamation?

Lincoln was not fully convinced that emancipation would be in the best interests concerning liberty to the slaves. He was giving the issue much thought and held it under advisement. As with any major decision, Lincoln proceeded slowly. Eventually, he did arrive at a decision.

Someone once said that life is a series of choices. We decide to get up out of bed in the morning, we decide to go to work, we decide to eat, we decide to sleep. All our actions, whether they be right or wrong, mundane or exciting; the fact is we make decisions all day everyday. In this fast paced hurried lifestyle which characterizes the "nineties," we tend to make hasty decisions. The key to decision making is to collect all the facts and proceed slowly. Once a decision has been derived, then it must be acted upon as soon as possible.

Abraham Lincoln was no fool.

THE FEAR OF THE LORD IS THE BEGINNING OF KNOWLEDGE, BUT FOOLS DESPISE WISDOM AND IN-STRUCTION (Proverbs 1:7). He was well aware and deeply believed that without God's favor, our highest wisdom is but as foolishness. He also knew that our most arduous efforts would avail nothing in the shadow of God's displeasure.

He counseled in prayer with the Almighty, before any final decisions were made. It may have appeared to us lowly mortals that it was an accident when Lincoln was elected to be the President of the United States. It was no accident! God is the one who ultimately determines who will lead nations. There is absolutely no question that Abraham Lincoln was the only man who could have been President at the time he was. No other individual could have lead our nation through the horrors of the Civil War. He was God fearing and applied the precepts of the Bible as a way of life. To this inspiration from God, we owe our nation!

TAKING THE GREAT HIGH ROAD

Edwin M. Stanton, Lincoln's Secretary of War, was accused by a major general of favoritism.

("THE HUMOROUS MR. LINCOLN," page 98) This accusation inscensed Stanton. He wrote a scathing reply. He took the letter to Lincoln and read it aloud. As he was reading, the President would frequently interrupt him by saying: "That's right, Stanton, give it to him. That's just what he deserves, good for you."

When Stanton finished his written harangue, he folded the letter and put it an envelope.

"What are you going to do with it now?" Linclon asked.

"Why send it, of course."

Don't do it, Stanton," Lincoln said.

"But you just said it was exactly what he deserved," Stanton replied.

"Yes," said Lincoln, "I believe he does deserve it, but you don't want to send such a letter as that. Put it in the fire. That's what I do when I get angry. It's a good letter, and you had a good time writing it and you feel better, don't you? It has done you good and answered its purpose. Now burn it."

What a wonderful lesson in wisdom. I took this maxim to heart, and applied it in my personal experience. There have been occasions in my life where I had felt slighted for whatever reason. My first reaction was to sit down and draft a hard-hitting, no holds barred type of letter. These letters have been some of my best work in writing, because the words came from my heart, harsh as they may have been at the time. The prose flowed and my purpose was very well explained and pointed. Upon completion, without exception, I would read my written remarks aloud. Now that all this poison was out of my system I would tear up the letter and toss it in the "circular file". I felt much better.

The above anecdote concerning Stanton, was excellent advice. Before the Civil War was over, Lincoln himself would have the opportunity to follow his own counsel. In July of 1863 the battle of Gettysburg was fought. It was not a battle site of choice for either side, but nevertheless it occurred. It was three days of the bloodiest and most vicious fighting of the war. It was hot. The participants were determined to break each other.

As we know from our history, the North prevailed. Lee's army was in total retreat. The Southern forces were in a classic predicament. Before Lee, was a swollen river his army could not cross. Behind him, was General Meade's Union army. An opportunity to engage and crush the Confederate army was at hand. Unfortunately, with the blown opportunity to crush Lee's army at Antietam, it appeared that once again, a second chance was apparently now being thrown away by the extreme caution of a general.

Lincoln became infuriated when he learned of this situation. Meade's apparent hesitation afforded sufficient time for General Lee to cross a receding river and escape total defeat. For over two long years, Lincoln had experienced and battled the frustration of dealing with generals who were too cautious. He proceeded to write a letter of severe reprimand to General Meade. Once again, being the man and having the presence of character, Lincoln gave it a second thought, and decided that it would do more harm than good to officially satisfy his frustration. He was soon to realize the wisdom of his decision, when he recieved a letter written by General Oliver O. Howard, who commanded a corps at Gettysburg, giving strong support to Meade. The three day battle had been so intense, nobody was in the mood to fight. Meade was a skilled and brave soldier. The battle of Gettysburg proved this. A Lincoln reprimand would have ruined a good general.

The lesson for us today, is that we need to put ourselves in other people's shoes before we are quick to criticize. How often does this happen in the home or the workplace? I've seen it happen all too often. The discretion of taking the great high road of leadership or serving selfish motivations, is a barometer and in direct relation to how well we exist as a society and a nation.

"FOUR SCORE AND SEVEN YEARS AGO..."

Lincoln's Gettysburg address is considered as one of the most effective speeches ever delivered. At the time, Lincoln did not think of it as a great speech. Maybe for him, it was just like falling off a log, but orators, politicians and platform speakers have been striving ever since to imitate its effectiveness.

The address contains all the elements of an effective presentation. First, is the attention getting opening. Lincoln reminds the people of the nation's heritage and purpose. Second, is the purpose of his address; can we as a nation live up to the foresight of our forefathers? Third, the main body of his speech focuses on the nation's business at hand, the civil war and what is at stake. Fourth, he concludes by reiterating our heritage and purpose as a nation and its importance to remain this way.

The most astounding aspect of Lincoln's Gettysburg Address, is that he delivered a complete speech power-packed with meaning and substance, and he did it by conveying the central idea of the occasion in about two minutes. What a model for future generations to emulate the clarity of thought and expressing that thought in the simplest of terms, a goal of which Lincoln constantly strove. Following this example in every aspect of communication, enlists the organization of thought and meaning. Abraham Lincoln learned very early, the wisdom of clear and concise communication.

"IF SLAVERY IS NOT WRONG, NOTHING IS WRONG."

Lincoln considereed himself anti-slavery. Why? Because it was and still is wrong! As President, he took an oath and agreed to the best of his ability to preserve, protect, and defend the Constitution of the United States. He also emphasized that he did not take the oath to gain power, and break the oath in using the power. What a noble concept for leadership. Another way of putting it is this: A leader should not seek the position in order to gain power, or break the sacred trust of those he or she is responsible for using that power. This is the precise reason the oppression of slavery and the slavery of oppression is WRONG! Selfish acquisition of power is abused power.

HUMAN NATURE WILL NOT CHANGE

When Lincoln was notified of his re-election in 1864, he read a prepared response from a window. In it, he explained that human nature does not change. ("THE LIVING LIN-

COLN," page 623) He believed that in any future national trial, there will be men who are weak, and as strong; as silly and as wise; as bad and good. He admonished that we need to study the incidents of this, as philosophy to learn wisdom and none of them as wrongs to be avenged.

With all the modern miracles of medicine and high technology, and whatever else has improved our lot on the physical plane, human nature does not change! The mixture of good and evil accounting for love and hate is the same now as it was when Cain slew Abel. History and events in the world today, along with our own individual circumstances continues to prove that — HUMAN NATURE DOES NOT CHANGE!

"WITH MALICE TOWARD NONE..."

On March 4, 1865 Lincoln delivered his Second Inaugural Address. It was a bleak day in Washington. The clouds were low in the sky, the wind blew a heavy gale, and carriage wheels sank in the mud on Pennsylvania Avenue. On the portico of the capitol, Lincoln delivered his address in a quiet voice. ("THE LIVING LINCOLN," page 638-640) President Lincoln retained his wisdom and humble frame of mind in spite of four years of tremendous rigor and stress his office demanded. The war was nearing its completion, and he realized that now was the time to inaugurate a campaign of reconciliation to heal the wounds of the nation. In a reflective tone he brought the nation back in time, when the controversy that plunged this nation into its bloodiest war, was about to commence. He mentioned that one party was trying to dissolve the Union peacefully, while the other was doing the same to preserve it. Both parties deprecated war, but one of them would make war rather than allow the nation to survive. The other would accept war rather than let it perish. The war came.

Neither party expected the magnitude and duration of the conflict. Both read the same Bible, and prayed to the same God. Lincoln still questioned the concept of any man to ask God's assistance in wringing their bread from the sweat of other men's faces. In the spirit of reconciliation, Lincoln cautioned the nation to "judge not that we be not judged."

The late Earl Curzon, Chancellor of Oxford University, declared Lincoln's address to be "the purest gold of human eloquence, nay of eloquence almost divine." ("LINCOLN THE UNKNOWN," Dale Carnegie, page 192) "It was like a sacred poem," he later wrote. "No ruler had ever spoken words like these to his people. America had never before had a president who had found such words in the depths of his heart."

The closing words of his speech have been estimated by this writer and others, to be the most noble and beautiful utterances ever delivered by the lips of mortal man.

> Fondly do we hope-fervently do we pray-that this mighty scourge of war may speedily pass away. Yet if God wills that it continue until all the wealth piled by the bondman's two hundred and fifty years or unrequited toil shall be sunk, and until every drop of blood drawn with the lash shall be paid by another drawn with the sword, as was said three thousand years ago, so still it must be said, "The judgements of the Lord are true and righteous altogether."
>
> With malice toward none; with charity to all; with firmness in the right, as God gives us to see the right, let us strive on to finish the work we are in; to bind up the nation's wounds; to care for him who shall have borne the battle, and for his widow, and his orphan—to all which may achieve and cherish a just and lasting peace among ourselves, and with all nations.

Two months later, to the day, this speech was read at Lincoln's funeral services in Springfield.

Lincoln's immortal utterances contained within his Second Inauguaral Address is a summation of the character of the man. As a true leader, he displayed honesty in telling it like it was. His candor concerning the motivations of the participants was haunting. The compassionate tone of reconciliation was heartening. His humor, although not evident in this speech, in times of great stress helped to take the edge off unbearable situations. The humility conveyed by the tone and content, exemplified a depth of character few have ever possessed. His Faith in God, that somehow all of what had transpired would work to the good, was unwavering. His love of family and of country were continously exemplified by his willingness to sacrifice his life for the benefit of both. His love of learning and applying what he learned, enabled him to acquire the wisdom that characterized his keenness of discernment and judgement.

There were many who heard the words Lincoln spoke. They thought they had listened to a prayer rather than a speech. Afterward, Walt Whitman saw Lincoln returning to the White House. He wrote: ("THE HUMOROUS MR. LINCOLN," page 137) "He was in his plain two-horse barouche, and looked very much worn and tired; the lines indeed, of vast responsibilities, intricate questions, and demands of life and death, cut deeper than ever upon his dark brown face; yet all the old goodness, tenderness, sadness and canny shrewdness underneath the furrows. (I never see that man without feeling that he is one to be attached to, for his combination of purest, heartiest, tenderness, and native Western form of manliness.) By his side sat his little boy of ten years. There were no soldiers, only a lot of civilians on horseback, with huge yellow scarfs over their shoulders, riding around the carriage. (At the inauguration four years ago, he rode down and back again surrounded by a dense mass of armed cavalryman, eight deep, with drawn sabers; and there were sharp-shooters stationed at every corner of the route.)"

What a difference four years can make. The contrast is remarkable. Imagine the positive difference we may incorporate in our lives by emulating the wisdom Lincoln learned to apply in his life. The man was loved by many!

GOOD LEADERSHIP COMFORTS AND UPLIFTS

Prior to the passage of the Emancipation Proclamation, there was much debate over the concept. Byron Sunderland, Chaplain of the Senate, called on the President when he heard a rumor concerning Lincoln's withdrawing the Emancipation Proclamation. The Chaplain gave good counsel. He mentioned to the President in his moment of indecision, that his master was the American people and should not deny them. Lincoln appreciated the advice, but remained torn as to the effect of freeing the slaves would have on the whites and blacks.

Chaplain Sunderland recollected that the ramifications of such a bold move caused Lincoln to recall a story he read in one of his first books, Aesop's Fables. In it, the text explained that four white men were scrubbing a Negro in a potash kettle filled with cold water. (THE HUMOROUS MR. LINCOLN," page 106-107)

By scrubbing the Negro, they figured he would become white. Right about the same time when they thought they were succeeding, the Negro took cold and died. "Now, I am afraid that by the time we get through with this war the Negro will take cold and die." History has shown, and contiues to display the fact that Lincoln's fear was well founded.

In a grave tone, Lincoln continued to discuss the question of emancipation. Sunderland said that Lincoln covered the issue in every light. His points were so clear, every statement was an argument. He showed with empathy each sides feeling. "It was like a talk of one of the old prophets," Sunderland said. "And though he did not tell me at the end whether the Proclamation would be issued or not, I went home comforted and uplifted, and I believed in Abraham Lincoln from that day."

President Lincoln wrangled over all aspects of an issue. He wanted to be absolutely sure he was about to do the right thing. His genuine and sincere desire to serve the American people was paramount. If our nation's leaders, and we as individuals continued this practice, many of the pitfalls we've encountered could have been avoided.

"A LITTLE MORE AND A LITTLE LESS NOISE."

As the war continued to go badly, Lincoln suffered no shortage of critics. To one man who really hounded Lincoln's Administration he offered the following story: ("THE HUMOROUS MR. LINCOLN," page 117).

"A traveler on the frontier found himself, as night came on, in a wild region. A terrible thunderstorm added to his trouble. He floundered along until the horse gave out. Occasional flashes of lightning afforded the only clue to the path, and the crashes of thunder were frightful. One bolt which seemed to crush the earth beneath him, made him stagger and brought him to his knees. Being by no means a praying man, his petition was short and to the point: 'Oh, Lord, if it's all the same to you, give us a little more light and a little less noise.'"

Isn't it true, that everyone is a critic? We are at our utmost of critiquing, when we are the least qualified. We are quick to forget and appreciate how it is to walk in another person's shoes. Sometimes, we criticize people or situations we don't know anything about. It makes much more sense, and is conducive to much more productivity, to shed light on a situation, rather than offer continual criticism.

SETTING THE RECORD STRAIGHT

The President suffered continual attacks of criticism. Many were unfounded. There were, however, some that were so vicious and unfounded that Lincoln was urged to set the record straight by sticking to the facts. ("THE HUMOROUS MR. LINCOLN," page 117) He always refused: "If I were to try to read, much less answer, all the attacks made upon me, this shop might just as well be closed for any other business. I do the very best I know how—the very best I can; and I mean to keep on going so until the end. If the end brings me out right, what is said against me won't amount to anything. If the end brings me out wrong, ten thousand angels swearing I was right wouldn't make any difference."

It requires courage to be a leader. We are all leaders in our own right. So, what Lincoln says applies to all of us. We must have the courage and conviction to do what is right! We must have the courage and fortitude to do the best we know how, and stick to it, resisting distractions. In the final analysis, it does not matter what others think. If you are right, what was said is of little value. If you happen to be wrong, the opposite holds true. All those who supported you, won't make any difference. The point is to hold fast to what is right! If you are proven wrong, then learn from it and move on.

LET'S SEE WHAT THE BOOK SAYS

Lincoln's wisdom was endless and also profound concerning the machinations of dealing with human nature. Where did he acquire and learn all this wisdom?

Two sons of Robert E. Lee were taken prisoner. They were held at Fortress Monroe awaiting execution in reprisal for the impending hanging of two Union officers. ("THE HUMOROUS MR. LINCOLN," page 134-136) Lee rushed to

Richmond requesting Jefferson Davis to intercede on behalf of his boys.

"You need not worry," Davis said. "Because Abraham Lincoln will not permit such an outrage.."

"Stanton will carry out his diabolical purpose," Lee replied. "And Lincoln will know nothing of it until it has been accomplished and both my sons are dead."

Davis prepared a telegram and had it sent through the lines to the White House. Lincoln read it and immediately summoned his Secretary of War, Stanton. Upon reading the telegram, Stanton advised the President that if the two Union officers were hanged in Richmond, then Lee's boys should be hanged in reprisal.

"Stanton," said the President. "If a crime is committed in Richmond I cannot prevent it, but a crime like that under my jurisdiction would stamp upon my heart, by command of my conscience, the word 'murderer.' Stanton, it can't be done...it can't be done...we are not savages."

Lincoln picked up a Bible from his desk and said: "Let us see what the Book says. Here is a command from Almighty God in His Book. Read these words yourself: 'Vengeance is mine; I will repay, saith the Lord.'"

The President wrote a message, signed it, and directed it be dispatched immediately to Fortress Monroe: "Immediately release both the sons of Robert E. Lee and send them back to their father."

What's in a name? What do people think of when a name is mentioned? It describes a person. In a instant, a person's reputation is called-up at the utterance of the name. Lincoln's reputation preceded him. In spite of the "bad blood" generated between Americans during the Civil War, a man's reputation and character remained paramount.

Jefferson Davis and Abraham Lincoln were politcal adversaries in the worst rendition of the term. It had been said that Lincoln's re-election was Davis' worst nightmare. Yet, Davis knew that Lincoln was an honorable man, and would not allow the outrage of "tit for tat" concerning Lee's sons and the two Union officers. It is extremely important to note that Lincoln did what was right! Regardless, if the two Union officers were killed, Lincoln would not be a party of perpetuating the madness of revenge. He put it in God's hands. Call it blind faith or sentmental buffoonery, but what Lincoln practiced, was that the beginning of knowledge and wisdom is the fear of the Lord. The key to Lincoln's wisdom and profound sense of leadership was derived from one of his favorite books, the Bible.

Chapter 9
Emulation

HOW CAN YOU BE LIKE LINCOLN?

Abraham Lincoln was an extraordinary man. He was original, fearless, and self-confident. His keen perceptions of right and wrong made him a leader and gave him an influence which most other men did not have. He rose above poverty and ignorance.

Lincoln carried his code of morals wherever he travelled in life. He refused to engage in schemes that were not credible. His wisdom was irrefutable. As a boy in Indiana he acquired a reputation for gentleness, kindness, and good-nature. He was unselfish and possessed a helpful disposition. His sympathetic nature and tender tact enabled him to give help without offense. He chopped wood for widows and stayed up all night to care for the sick. While living at the Rutledge Tavern, he was always willing to give up his bed for a traveller. He was never so happy as when he was doing good. That was his religion.

Lincoln was a religious man, but did not subscribe to a particular faith. He was wise enough to know and follow the precepts set forth in the Bible as it was written, rather than depending on theological interpretation. There was no question that he be believed in Divine Providence. His reasoning and decision making was based on his desire to please God. In one of his speeches he said:

"I know that the Lord is always on the side of the right; but it is my constant anxiety and prayer that I and this nation should be on the Lord's side." (THE TRUE ABRAHAM LINCOLN," William Eleroy Curtis, P:382)

He believed in the efficacy of prayer. Tears filled Lincoln's eyes when a visitor mentioned that the people of the north were giving all they had, which included their sons as well as their confidence and prayers. Lincoln's greatness was dominated by his absolute self-control. The character traits outlined in this writing would not have been possible otherwise. Honesty was his policy of behavior in dealing with others. The application of candor promoted an air of clarity which garnered the respect of many. The development of compassion enabled him to possess a keen sense of feeling for the suffering. Without this, the Emancipation Proclamation would have been just one more, in a series of, feel-good political band-aids that would have faded into oblivion. His use of humor took the edge off things. His penchant for melancholy was well known. He sought the lighter side of life in order to offset the rigors of living. Lincoln's use of humor was not only therapeutic for himself, but served as a valuable salve for all who were fortunate to partake of it. Humility was key to his greatness because he never forgot his frontier roots. His attitude did not change or become puffed-up, regardless of his station in life. Whether a rail splitter or President of the United States, ol' Abe remained the same. His faith in God and that the cause of right would prevail, was unshakable. The combination of the above contributed to his devoted love of family and country. Through crude experience and the life-long love of learning, he possessed a level of wisdom instrumental in saving a nation. The character of Lincoln enabled him to become one of the greatest leaders of all time. When he entered the Presidency, Lincoln felt inadequate for his responsibilities. When he saw his duty, however, he did it with courage, endurance, magnanimity, and unselfish devotion. In his eulogy of Lincoln, shortly after his assassination, Ralph Waldo Emerson said:

"He grew according to the need; his mind mastered the problem of the day; and as the problem grew so did his comprehension of it. Rarely was a man so fitted to the event.

"In four years— four years of battle days—his endurance, his fertility and resources, his magnanimity, were sorely tried and never found wanting. There, by his courage, his justice, his even temper, his fertile counsel, his humanity, he stood a heroic figure in the centre of an heroic epoch."

We, sooner or later, as individuals in are own right, will face similar challenges. Was Lincoln superhuman? No, he was not! He did the best he could with what he had. He was not a rich man in the material sense, but he possessed tremendous wealth in the area of character. We too are capable of possessing this wealth.

As a great leader of a nation, a family, and himself, the binding component of Lincoln's greatness lies within his willingness to have esteemed others more highly than himself. Therein is the key to leadership. Is it possible to become great like Lincoln? The answer is yes! By applying the principals set forth in this book, anyone is capable of achieving the level of greatness attained by Abraham Lincoln.

Lincoln did not do or accomplish anything in his life that no other person could have accomplished. It is true that he possessed certain talents and exemplified strength of character, which propelled him to a high standard of existence. In spite of this, he was merely a human being. The question is: Are you willing to exert the effort required, in order to realize your potential?

We are continually exposed to lifelong opportunities enabling us to be leaders in our own right. A leader is a person who cares enough to change the circumstances which are hurting people. Lincoln did it as an individual and as the President of the United States. YOU can do it as an individual in your family, in the workplace, and as a member of society. President John F. Kennedy, in his Inaugural Address asked the following question which has been immortalized.

"Ask not what your country can do for you, but ask what you can do for your country." As leaders in our own right, and being motivated to change the circumstances which are hurting people, let us continually ask the following question: "How can I make your day more pleasant?"

Chapter 10
A Leader Leads

A good working definition of a leader is a person who leads. By definition a leader guides by the hand, or conducts by showing the way. The leader shows the method by which to attain a goal. To be an effective leader, one must be an effective manager who leads.

In July of 1864, Lincoln accepted the resignation of Salmon P. Chase as his Secretary of the Treasury. The cabinet post went to William Pitt Fessenden of Maine, who had been the chairman of the Senate Finance Committee. The appointment came with some practical counsel. (THE LIVING LINCOLN," Page 609)

THE SAFETY OF CONSULTATION
In his view of the daily operations of the Cabinet, Lincoln believed that in questions affecting the whole country, there should be full and frequent consultations. He advised that nothing should be done particularly affecting any department without consultation with the head of that Department.

The above is an excellent management principal. A leader in any facet, should continually seek consultation with no decisions made until the counsel of those directly involved in implementing the decision are advised. The old saying pertaining to the f act that there is safety within the counsel of many holds true. This does not mean that one requires permission or needs to consult with everyone under the sun, in order to arrive at a decision. Not at all. It merely means that a leader is wise to consult with those who can and are directly involved with the execution of the decision. This can apply to a CEO of a giant corporation or the husband of a household.

THE ART OF EVALUATION
A good leader is a good manager and evaluator. Once again, I must stress that when I refer to the role of leadership, this means YOU the reader. The following principal of leadership may apply to everyone, regardless of the situation.

In January of 1863, Lincoln placed Major General Hooker as the head of the Army of the Potomac. (THE LIVING LINCOLN," Page 535) He believed the decision was based on sufficient reasons. He did, however, recognize the fact that Hooker had shortcomings. Notice how Lincoln handles this situation in the following letter he penned to Hooker:

I have placed you at the head of the army of the Potomac. Of course I have done this upon what appear to me to be sufficient reasons. And yet I think it best for you to know that there are some things in regard to which, I am not quite satisfied with you. I believe you to be a brave and a skillful soldier, which of course, I like. I also believe you do not mix politics with your profession, in which you are right. You have confidence in yourself, which is valuable, if not an indispensable quality. You are ambitious, which, within reasonable bounds, does good rather than harm. But I think that during Gen. Burnside's command of the army, you have taken counsel of your ambition, and thwarted him as much as you could, in which you did great wrong to the country, and to a most meritorious and honorable brother officer. I have heard, in such way as to believe it, of your recently saying that both the army and government need a dictator.

Of course it was not for this, but in spite of it, that I have given you the command. Only those generals who gain successes, can set up dictators. What I now ask of you is military success, and I will risk the dictatorship. The government will support you to the utmost of its ability, which is neither more or less than it has done and will do for all commanders. I much fear that the spirit which you have aided to infuse into the army, of criticizing their commander, and withholding confidence from him, will now turn upon you. I shall assist you as far as I can, to put it down. Neither you, nor Napoleon, if he were alive again, could get any good out of an army, while such a spirit prevails in it. And now, beware of rashness. Beware of rashness, but with energy, and sleepless vigilance, go forward, and give us victories.

Lincoln was a master in dealing with people. A proper evaluation should always begin by pointing out a person's positive attributes. This is evidenced by Lincoln's opening remarks to Hooker. He then proceeded to point out, with candor and honesty, Hooker's shortcomings and what he needed to do to improve his performance. Then, Lincoln told him exactly what he expected of him as a commander. He wanted military success. Finally, Lincoln cautioned against rashness, which appeared to be Hooker's greatest flaw as a leader. Lincoln repeated the caution for emphasis and clarity of thought expressed in the simplest of terms. In summary, a proper evaluation of a subordinate by a manager or a leader should be as follows:

1. Point out the positive attributes of the one being evaluated.

2. Point out the areas needing improvement.

3. Explain candidly and honestly, in simple terms, how to improve upon the shortcomings.

4. Offer support in order to help the person realize what is expected.

5. Give one final bit of advice, and reiterate what is expected.

TAKING THE CIRCLE OUT OF THE SQUARE

In 1863 General Hooker was relieved of Command of the Army of the Potomac. The reason, he simply was not getting the job done. Hooker was a good soldier who was willing to fight, but when he was given command of the entire army, it became apparent that he had exceeded his bounds of competency. This did not mean, however, that he was good for nothing. Lincoln, being the consummate leader, recognized this. He did not allow personalities or ego stroking to get in the way of getting the overall job done.

To make the best use of Hooker as opposed to merely discarding him, Lincoln forwarded a communication to General Meade asking him if it would be agreeable, with all things considered, for Hooker to take a corps under him. Lincoln assured Meade of the strictest confidence in this matter and wanted an honest reply from Meade before he would approach Hooker. (THE LIVING LINCOLN," Page 566)

What can we learn from Lincoln's sound management in 1863, which we can glean today? First, Lincoln realized the value of a good employee. Often, in the corporate world, a person is elevated to a higher position of authority or management, and they fall flat on their face. They have exceeded their level of competency. In the corporate world, most middle or upper management personnel who fail, do so because they are not really cut out for the position to which they were promoted.

Lincoln understood the value of an employee. He knew that in Hooker's case, he would be valuable to him in another capacity. Why? Because he already proved himself. Hooker failed as an army commander, but not as a corps commander. Why is it that in the corporate world especially, when a person exceeds his her level of competency, they are thrown out completely? What a shame! What a waste of good talent!

Second, please notice that Lincoln had the common decency to ask Meade's thoughts on the prospect of Hooker serving under him. He didn't force General Hooker onto Meade. Lincoln always operated with respect and consulted with his subordinates before rendering an important decision. Lincoln simply cared for his people.

A GOOD PRACTICE

In November of 1862, the war was not going well for the North. An aggressive, take-charge sort of general eluded Lincoln's need for a commander to win some victories in the field. He was frustrated at this prospect, but maintained his composure:

"I certainly have been dissatisfied with the slowness of Buell and McClellan; but before I relieved them I had great fears I should not find successors to them, who would do better; and I am sorry to add, that I have seen little since to relieve those fears."

Good advice for managers today. If you have an employee that is unsatisfactory, but tolerable in the short term, it is

141

wise to be patient and find a replacement first, before terminating the associate. In my experiences and observances, I have witnessed many occasions where an employee was terminated prematurely, thereby causing a strain on the remainder of the staff, ultimately suffering the entire operation.

If an employee has committed a major infraction, which calls for immediate dismissal, then so be it. For example, it is not prudent to remove a marginal associate who happens to be the only one who knows the bookkeeping procedure in the entire work force. Get the point?

BEING ABLE TO ADMIT THE PROSPECT OF BEING WRONG

Another mark of an outstanding leader, regardless of one's position in life, is the ability and security of one's character to admit they may be wrong at times. Lincoln possessed this ability. In the following letter to Major General McClellan, dated October 27, 1862, (THE LIVING LINCOLN," Page 508) demonstrates Lincoln's willingness to give a person some space and admit the possibility of being wrong:

Yours of yesterday received. Most certainly I intended no injustice to any; and if I have done any, I deeply regret it. To be told after more than five weeks total inaction of the army, and during which period we had sent to that army every fresh horse we possibly could, amounting in the whole to 7,918, that the cavalry horses were too much fatigued to move, presented a very cheerless, almost hopeless, prospect for the future; and it may have forced something of impatience into my despatches. If not recruited, and rested then, when could they ever be? I suppose the river is rising, and I am glad to believe you are crossing.

There are occasions, when it is prudent as a leader, in whatever capacity, to give someone the benefit of the doubt.

EXAMINING THE PROS AND CONS

In September of 1862 the concept of emancipation was a burning issue. In principal and legality Lincoln did not have any problems with it, but there remained many unanswered questions. In spite of the fact that he decided earlier to issue the proclamation, he continued to argue the matter as if it were still an open question:

Do not misunderstand me, because I have mentioned these objections. They indicate the difficulties that have thus far prevented my action in some such way as you desire. I have not decided against a proclamation of liberty to the slaves, but hold the matter under advisement. And I can assure you that the subject is on my mind, by day and night, more than any other. Whatever shall appear to be God's will I will do. I trust that, in the freedom with which I have canvassed your views, I have not in any respect injured your feelings. (THE LIVING LINCOLN," Page 503)

A good manager or leader will examine the pros and cons of a matter before rendering a decision. All aspects of the issue must be examined in the best interest of all those concerned. Those who are familiar with the game of chess, well understand the danger of making a move on the board, before considering all the possible ramifications of such a decision.

STATING A POSITION

In August of 1862, Horace Greely, unleashed a bitter editorial attack in the *New York Tribune*, concerning the policy Lincoln pursued regarding the slaves of rebels. There were nine specific accusations fostering the opinion that the President was as way off base concerning the emancipation provisions of the new Confiscation Act. Remembering his earlier goal to express clarity of thought in its simplest of terms, Lincoln replied in a moderate tone, but his position was very clear. That position was to save the Union. Whatever was required to do or not do, to achieve this end, Lincoln intended no modification concerning his personal wish that all men everywhere could be free.

It is so important for a person in a leadership position to have a clear and concise stated purpose. How can people follow someone who is drifting in the sea of confusion and murky intents? It is essential for a leader to state his or her position on a matter. The worst thing that can be said of a leader is that "we don't know what he stands for!"

An effective leader must have the courage to state a position with conviction, no matter what the consequences.

HOW TO HANDLE A PROBLEM EMPLOYEE

Civil War buffs are well aware of Lincoln's frustration with his generals early in the war, because they failed to act with any amount of decisiveness.

Major General McClellan drove him crazy in this regard. Here's how Lincoln handled the situation.

Your despatches complaining that you are not properly sustained, while they do not offend me, do pain me very much. There is a curious mystery about the number of troops now with you. When I telegraphed you on the 6th saying you had over 100,000 with you, I had just obtained from the Secretary of War, a statement, taken as he said, from your own returns, making 108,000 then with you, and en route to you. You now say you will have but 85,000, when all en route to you shall have reached you. How can the discrepancy of 23,000 be accounted for?

And, once more let me tell you, it is indispensable to you that you strike a blow. I am powerless to help this. You will do me the justice to remember I always insisted, that going down the Bay in search of a field, instead of fighting at or near Manassas, was only shifting, and not surmounting, a difficulty—that we should find the same enemy, and the same, or equal, entrenchments, at either place. The country will not fail to note—is now noting—that the present hesitation to move upon an entrenched enemy, is but the story of Manassas repeated.

I beg to assure you that I have never written you, or spoken to you, in greater kindness of feeling than now, nor with a fuller purpose to sustain you, so far as in my most anxious judgement, I consistently can. But you must act. (THE LIVING LINCOLN," Page 471)

The point is this. Lincoln had a tremendous problem concerning the lack of respect from his people. His generals maligned him for his apparent lack of military knowledge. He learned fast , however, and was not intimidated when it came time to correct General McClellan. He stated his position clearly and confidently, wanting to know why certain things were not getting done. The same holds true today . If you find yourself in a similar situation, and I've been there myself, you have to come across with knowledge of what you're doing and demand some answers. Notice, though, Lincoln always allowed a man his dignity. Lincoln could be blunt at times, which was fine if the situation warranted it, but never stripped away a person's dignity. If you wish to continue being a respected and effective leader, never ever strip a person of their dignity. Eventually, Lincoln won the respect and admiration of an entire nation. He was a "class act," and that's why he is our most revered President.

"LEAST SAID, SOONEST MENDED"

President Lincoln believed in fair play, and backed up his subordinates when they were wronged. The following reply to Brig. General S. R. Curtis on December 12, 1861 explains:

I snatch a moment to both thank you, and apologize to you. In all sincerity I thank you for the complete and entirely satisfactory manner in which you executed the trusts I confided to you by letter.

You, and others, particularly, and the public service generally, were wronged, and injured by the publication of General Thomas' report, on his return from the West. I have no apology only to say it never would have been done, if I had had the least suspicion it was to be done. Being done,

I thought the maxim "Least said, soonest mended" applied to the case. Yours very truly.

This is a clear case where an employee was wronged, and there was nothing that could be done about it. Acknowledging the infraction and advising to move on as quickly as possible is more often than not, the better course of action.

THOUGHTFULNESS

Abraham Lincoln continually gave priority to the welfare of others. If someone were short on cash or in some sort of bind, even if they were a stranger, he would come to their aid. His thoughtfulness for others is best exemplified with his thoughts on marriage contained in a letter he wrote to his friend Mary Owens, as a young man in 1837.

"Whatever woman may cast her lot with mine, should any ever do so, it is my intention to do all in my power to make her happy and contented; and there is nothing I can imagine, that would make me more unhappy, than to fail in the effort..."

Eventually, Lincoln would marry in November 1842, to Mary Todd. He thought it to be a matter of profound wonderment. He would have a lifelong opportunity to put into practice, his desire to make his woman happy. His wonderful and sincere implementation of leadership skills as a husband and a father are chronicled in a preceding chapter dealing with love of family and country.

MAXIMUM PARTICIPATION

Lincoln was a leader who led. He possessed many skills and utilized them. This is sound advice for us. In closing for this particular chapter, I want to share with you, one more management principal that was mentioned to me by a dear friend of mine as we conversed over this book. My friend Mary is a retired employee from the telephone company. Part of her experience on the management side of the company, was to mediate disputes or grievances between the labor union and management.

She was successful at mediation. I asked her why? "The key," she said, "was maximum participation. Get them involved in arriving at a solution among themselves." Mary went on to say that it is very important to LISTEN as the engaging parties share ideas. "By listening to what is said, you can then guide the group to an agreeable solution," she said. "The worst thing one could do in a mediation session is to get in the middle of the c controversy." She stressed that it is more effective and less stressful for everyone concerned to stand back and allow the debating parties to work out their own problems.

Maximum participation, getting people involved, and a MUST LISTEN approach to understanding different points of view are essential ingredients to successful leadership in any situation.

Chapter 11
Charting the Great High Road Course

The mark of a great leader is one who continually sets attainable goals. There are short and long term goals. Short term goals are self-imposed tasks to be completed in the near future, usually up to six months in duration. Long term goals may take up to a year or longer to accomplish. Within each category, it is extremely important to chart, in writing, a daily course by which to arrive at the forecasted destination. That's right! All your goals should be in writing! Make a record of it. Goals in your mind are merely dreams. Writing them down is the first step to making them a reality. It is also important that these goals be realistic in approach. We tend to bite off more than we can chew, or set

148

our sights too high. Being realistic and patient are keys to success in attaining goals. Striving to attain goals is paramount to realizing constant improvement in our lives, regardless of our individual situations.

If you've gotten this far, I hope you are pleased and inspired by what you've read, and are ready to take action. The only question remaining, is what can you do now in the way of goal setting to chart a course on the great high road of your life? It will require planning of a daily, weekly, monthly, and yearly strategy to incorporate the character-istics discussed in this work, in order to achieve what few others had the courage to master.

Several more questions before you begin. Do you really and honestly desire, with every fiber of your being, the true greatness that characterized Abraham Lincoln? As a leader in your own right, are you ready to be sensitive to other people's needs, especially those closest to you? Are you tired and fed up of just being average? Are you ready to pursue what you were cut out for? Part of what made Lincoln great, was the fact that he did what he liked and was skilled at it. He desired to be a politician. He was good at it, he liked it, and as a result, he was able to handle the challenges of his chosen vocation.

If you answer yes to these questions, you are ready to begin the quest of travelling on a higher plane of existence. It's not too late to begin. There is no age limit to embark on a path of positive character building that can put you in the same league as Lincoln.

When setting your individual goals in this regard, be ever mindful of this most important principal: Esteem others higher than yourself!

Without genuine concern for others, setting goals for incorporating the character building components I out-lined in this book are doomed to failure. A sincere heart is required, and sensitivity to the needs of others. In order for the trait of integrity to be incorporated into one's daily activity, the power of doing good must be developed.

Honesty is truly the best policy over the long haul. This one does require patience. In this world of one-upsmanship, it is increasingly difficult to walk the straight and narrow. Straight and narrow we must walk. Take one day at a time. Getting through the next 24 hours is plenty long enough to set your sights for now. Be aware and sensitive to situations that pop up, which challenge your honesty. There is no situation too small or insignificant by which to begin. Even if the cashier gave you a penny too much in change or the waiter forgot to add the dessert on your restaurant bill, be honest and do the right thing. Corny, you bet! If you want to be known as HONEST (your name), and be in the same class as Lincoln, then you know what must be done.

Candor, as we have learned is a powerful tool in the art of communication. Plain speech is essential to success in leadership. Lincoln was a master of being perfectly frank with his subordinates. Candor clears the air. Everyone knows what you are talking about. The margin of misunderstanding or miscommunication is greatly diminished when the pains of candor are exacted. Wars, divorces, law suits, and many other problems can be avoided by employing candor. A word of caution, however -- being that candor is a powerful tool, it should not be utilized as a weapon. This book is not dedicated to the fallacy of intimidation, but the art of consideration.

Compassion is a characteristic which is best learned through suffering. How can a person in a position of leadership (that means all of us) empathize with someone if that person has absolutely no clue as to what the other person is experiencing ? It is a well documented fact that Lincoln suffered greatly. How else could he have a fellow feeling for the suffering? How could he empathize with the oppression of the slaves? Understanding how it feels to "walk a mile in another person's shoes," require s compassion.

A person who would be a leader in the same vein as Lincoln, would supplement compassion with action. Feeling sorry for someone does no good unless something is done to rectify the situation.

Humor was a unique and valuable tool for success in Lincoln's leadership. He had been maligned for the use of his humor. The "stuffed shirts" of the time had no sense of humor under the best of conditions. They continually misunderstood his intent .

A leader is wise to employ the use of humor, especially under stressful conditions because it takes the edge off tension. Lincoln was also a master at this. His humor had a purpose. He never exposed his listeners to frivolity.

There is a lesson for us today concerning humor. At the appropriate time, humor is beneficial and can strengthen the resolve for those it is intended. Frivolity or saying things in jest, has no purpose. Utilizing humor to make a point or send a message emulates one of the characteristics that made Lincoln great.

Humility is indeed a peculiar ambition. Of all the characteristics required for integrity discussed in this book, humility seems to be among the least fashionable in today's modern philosophy. We remain in the "me first" mode of thinking . The current educational philosophy for pre-schoolers stresses that the little toddlers act aggressively on their own behalf. Children are not being taught how to respect others. They are being brainwashed early on to rely on themselves, care for themselves , and forget everybody else.

What will our society be like in the near future without humility? Unfortunately, the near future has already arrived. Crime in just about every category is up. Why? Teen pregnancy is at epidemic proportions. Why? Abortions are being performed at an indiscriminate rate. Why? Adultery and fornication are practically accepted practices in society. Why? The divorce rate in marriages continues at an unacceptable high rate. Why? Domestic violence and child abuse abounds. Why? The haughty attitude of star athletes and high-powered business professionals is an accepted form of hero worship. If the peculiar ambition of humility were prevalent in society, there would be no need to ask these questions.

The main lesson we can learn from Lincoln's humble approach to life is this: A person who is truly humble in every aspect of their life will be exalted. Lincoln epitomized this concept. His classic example of true humility exalted him from his meager beginnings in Kentucky to the Presidency of the United States of America. What happened to all those haughty rivals Lincoln encountered in his path of life? Without exception, all those who sought exaltation were abased!

True humility is a strength not a weakness. The modern connotation of the word denotes a person who has no backbone, or as we used to say when I was kid, "a jellyfish." This is far from the truth. A person who is humble is not a coward. A person who is humble is one who does not place himself or herself more important than anyone else. We all have one thing in common. We are human beings. Nothing more, nothing less. We are all born, and one day we are to die. It doesn't matter how haughty, rich, or important one feels they may be, we all die! The ultimate question is: What can I do to develop the power of doing good for my neighbor in my life? Not, what can I do to "grab for all the gusto I can," and walk over everyone before I kick-off? This is what humility is all about. Knowing one's place in the scheme of creation. Knowing, that one day we will all be accountable to a higher power for what the fruit of our actions rendered in this short life.

Faith is the assurance of hope not yet realized. Lincoln had faith in the fact that if he did what was right presently, the future would bring back the same in kind. Faith is knowing that somehow all things will work to the good, provided the proper steps are taken. It's the assurance of hope that is to become a future reality.

Lincoln put faith to the test in his life many times (see chapter 6). Without exception, he acted reasonably and with foreknowledge concerning his faith actions.

Does this mean that one should act in "blind faith." Absolutely not! This is what has given faith a bad rap. Too many people in positions of authority and influence have coerced, deceived, manipulated, and intimidated trusting souls into blind faith.

What a tragedy. Honest, law-abiding, and trusting souls have been physically and spiritually raped. If you are a victim of this type of diabolical action, take heart and don't give up on the faith of what is right and true. These predators will be dealt with harshly in their due time. So hang-in, and keep the faith!

Love of family and of country is paramount to our survival as a nation. What is love anyway? I believe that love is an act of out-flowing concern without conditions. Too often in this life I see the appearance of love, but it is really self-love . There are conditions attached to the act. Think about your own life and actions of love. Do you show acts of love in order to get something in return? If you do, that is not love, but greed. The motivation of self indulgence under the guise of love is one of the biggest cons we foster upon ourselves and each other. How can we say we are loving each other, if when you get right down to it, we are usually looking out for ourselves?

As human beings we are all created with free moral agency. That is to say a free will. We have the power to choose. We can choose to be kind, or we can choose to be evil. Ultimately, in every case, the choice remains ours to make. The act of true love is an attitude. Are we genuinely concerned with each other's welfare? This is the key to love! If one possesses the sincere desire to develop the power of doing good, that person will extend love in the way it was intended: ESTEEMING OTHERS HIGHER THAN SELF!

How does one develop the power of doing good? For a detailed explanation, reread this entire book. It begins with honesty with oneself and others. Being candid and compassionate tells others you really do care for their welfare. Utilizing humor at the appropriate time makes everyone's life more bearable. Being humble and faithful sets an example that in the long run, people will admire and respect. Exacting true love in every aspect of our daily activity is the ultimate challenge of human interaction. It requires a lifetime of perfecting. It is worth it, because without love, we are all doomed!

Wisdom results when the seven character traits discussed in this book are mastered. A knowledge derived from experience in the road of life diminishes the victimization of evil and deception which permeates this sad world of ours. There are certain things about this existence which are out of our control to change. No one human being can alter this world. That is a simple fact. That's why when a politician promises change and a better life for all, as a result of their election, it is simple deception. Certainly, it is worthy to strive to improve our lot, however, without true love, all our travail is an exercise in futility.

Taking the great high road in all our actions is noble and required for survival. Who are you? Why are you here? What is your potential? You are a wonderful creation. A masterpiece which is unequalled in this physical universe. You are here in this life to begin on the road of realizing your full potential as that masterpiece. Understanding this, your potential as a person within the framework of taking the great high road of leadership in your own right, is UNLIMITED! Incorporating and applying the character building components discussed in this book can only work if they are bound by a common thread. That thread is the continual act of esteeming others more highly than oneself, or considering others first. The time is rapidly approaching when ALL of us as human beings will have the wonderful opportunity to achieve our unlimited potential!

The end for now!

References Cited

Angle & Miers. THE LIVING LINCOLN, Barnes & Noble Books, New York, 1992.

Carnegie, Dale. LINCOLN THE UNKNOWN, Dale Carnegie & Assocs., Garden City, NY, 1903.

Curtis, William E. THE TRUE ABRAHAM LINCOLN, J.B. Lippincott Co., Philadelphia, PA, 1903.

Jennison, Keith W. THE HUMOROUS MR. LINCOLN, Thomas Y. Corwell Co., New York, NY, 1965.

Emerson, Ralph W. COMPLETE WRITINGS, Wm. H. Wise Co., New York, NY, 1929.